Smashed Avocado

Smashed Avocado

How I cracked the property market and you can too

Nicole Haddow

NERO

Published by Nero,
an imprint of Schwartz Books Pty Ltd
Level 1, 221 Drummond Street
Carlton VIC 3053, Australia
enquiries@blackincbooks.com
www.blackincbooks.com

9781760641498 (paperback)
9781743821114 (ebook)

 A catalogue record for this
book is available from the
National Library of Australia

Cover design by Josh Durham, Design by Committee
Cover illustrations by Georgia Norton-Lodge
Avos of wisdom illustrations by Jojoba
Text design and typesetting by Tristan Main

Printed in Australia by McPherson's Printing Group.

NOTE TO READERS

This publication contains the opinions and ideas of its author. It is sold with
the understanding that neither the author nor the publisher is engaged in rendering
legal, tax, investment, insurance, financial, accounting, or other professional advice
or services. If the reader requires such advice or services, a competent professional
should be consulted. Relevant laws vary from state to state. The strategies outlined
in this book may not be suitable for every individual, and are not guaranteed or
warranted to produce any particular results.

No warranty is made with respect to the accuracy or completeness of the
information contained herein, and both the author and publisher specifically
disclaim any responsibility for any liability, loss or risk, personal or otherwise,
which is incurred as a consequence, directly or indirectly, of the use and
application of any of the contents of this book.

To Joel, for being home

Contents

1

The Wake-Up Call

I STOOD IN THE SHALLOW water of my friend Kate's pool, sinking flutes of bubbles and celebrating the arrival of the big three zero. It was a perfect summer day in December 2012, and I was thrilled to be surrounded by my closest friends. The Instagram pictures reveal happy, tanned girls living the dream. I was wearing Gucci sunglasses and a designer bikini. I hadn't dared get my high-maintenance haircut wet.

It was all a carefully constructed lie. Behind my wide, champagne-induced grin, there was a mind utterly consumed with the previous decade's indulgent lifestyle, which had rendered me completely broke. More than broke, actually. I'd racked up a stupid amount of debt attempting to pose as an adult.

It started with sharehousing. For young people, sharehouses are a rite of passage. Finally, we're freed from the shackles of parental rule. We come home drunk and it's celebrated rather than discouraged. We have sex without questions or judgement. Sharehouses mean so much more than the cost of rent paid to a wealthy baby boomer. It's that time in our lives when the struggle is still kind of fun. We navigate the end of adolescence and take those first tentative steps into 'adulting'. We're still dodging the serious responsibilities of grown-up life, while embracing the fun bits. The freedom of eating a packet of potato chips for dinner trumps the stress of learning how to manage income. If your housemate had a shit day, you hit a bar and help them drown their sorrows. You throw parties and make enough cheap punch to fill a bath.

The first time I moved out was at twenty-three, when I journeyed overseas on a whim. I was sitting in my parents' study, doing some research into an ex-boyfriend's relationship status. (This was the pre-Facebook era, so I had to use other avenues to find out what he was up to.) A comprehensive search revealed that he'd happily moved on and I dealt with this by drinking the best part of a bottle of red wine from my parents' stash. 'Just get on a plane!' a friend who'd moved to Geneva advised in an instant message. Halfway through my fourth glass, I booked a one-way ticket to Europe.

I funded this trip with $6000 in credit the bank had merrily given me because I had worked full-time for a measly six months in retail between university degrees (I'd acquired a massive HECS debt too). The credit was far more than anyone my age should have been given: the moment the plastic had landed in my hand, I'd dropped a grand on designer sunnies and a handbag. And now, in a moment of gloominess heightened by shiraz, I'd spontaneously financed a trip to Europe as well.

Fast-forward nine months. I was devouring some overpriced Mykonos calamari when my mum called. 'The bank rang,' she said. 'It's probably time to come home.' Despite working as an au pair – a role that required me to care for a two-year-old boy in a rent-free home on the French-Swiss border – and trying to be careful with my spending, I'd powered through all my credit taking weekend ski trips and mini breaks in other locations. A few weeks after Mum's call, I used my emergency funds to wing my way back to Australia.

Attempting serious adulting round one

I returned to Australia with nothing but a suitcase full of dirty clothes, some wild travel tales and debt. I paid off only a tiny part of that before moving in with friends in a semi-detached South Melbourne terrace. It was considered cheap. My share was just $715 per month. At this point, I was twenty-five, earning $45,000 in an entry-level media job, writing copy for hotel guides and custom travel publications. I was making the minimum credit card repayments and also trying to keep up with my mates. We lived directly across the road from a pub and I spent too many hours perched at its bar sipping sauv blanc to save a thing. Needless to say, the amount owing on the card hovered constantly around the limit, and everything that landed in my account swiftly exited again.

I met a bloke. He lived next door to the pub across the road. We built a friendship kicking a footy back and forth in the street. Soon we were dating – if you could call it that. Mostly we drank and gambled. If we weren't at the racetrack, we were sitting in a pub watching the ponies on a big screen, plugging each-way bets into his Sportsbet account. I'd always enjoyed the occasional flutter. Getting dressed up, sitting on the lawn in the sun drinking champagne and potentially pocketing enough for a new pair of shoes felt like a very adult way to spend a Saturday. But my picks were usually based on the horse's name or how pretty it was, so the wins were rare. It took far too long to realise I was losing more than money.

I'd traded ambition for comfort. Although I felt too young to worry about buying a home, I definitely wanted one, and presumably to achieve that would require a successful career. My boyfriend was different – happy to live in the now, rent his digs and enjoy a stress-free job. I suppressed any thoughts and concerns about the future, because seriously dealing with our differences would mean going our separate ways, and I wasn't ready for that. I liked being one half of a couple, and I was having a lot of fun.

But soon my hunger for more rose to the surface. My boyfriend had no desire to travel. I did. I booked a solo trip to New York. I funded the flight with my second credit card, which came with a fresh $5000 limit. I justified it because I had lined up an interview there with the vice-president of Christie's auction house; it was for a writing assignment, which made at least part of the trip tax-deductible.

On the day of the interview, I arrived early. I was ushered into a small room where meticulously groomed women were pawing at jewellery that would soon go to auction. 'Try this,' a staff member with a thick American accent suggested, gesturing to a necklace sitting on a puffy velvet cushion. 'Oh, I'm just here for a meeting,' I replied. She smiled, carefully unclipped the clasp and placed it around my neck anyway. 'A quarter of a million,' she gushed, holding up the mirror. I stared at the diamonds and sapphires hanging heavily on my collarbone. In this surreal New York moment, I got my fire back – my career suddenly rocketed to the top of my agenda. I had always dreamed of writing features for magazines, which I knew might require a move interstate, but in settling into a relationship I'd temporarily let that aspiration go. Now, the desire to pursue that dream again felt too strong to ignore. It was better than watching a long-shot horse race to victory. The time had come to back *myself*.

Newly inspired, after my New York trip, I moved to Sydney to work for fashion magazines. On my own. At twenty-seven, I felt like I'd finally made it – even though I was juggling unstable freelance and contract gigs, while carrying $8000 in credit card debt. When I moved into a two-storey, double-fronted four-bedroom terrace in Potts Point, I lied about having a secure income to win the $1200-per-month room. I was hustling hard to land commissions to write features. My social media updates included links to articles in *Madison* and *Cleo*. When I scored a stint writing content for *The X Factor*'s website, I posted behind-the-scenes pics from the studio and happy snaps with Ronan

Keating. Those peering into the edited, digital version of my days could be forgiven for believing I was having the time of my life. I thought I was – these were pivotal moments in my career. The fact that it was costing me more than I was earning was insignificant. At least, that's what I told myself. I constantly found ways to justify it: you have to spend money to make money, right?

When I wasn't working, I was hanging out with my housemates: a lawyer, an investment banker and a town planner. They earned substantially more than I did, but they were my social lifeline, so if they went out I went with them. I faked cool indifference when dinner bills arrived, whacking my share on whichever of my credit cards wasn't completely maxed out. Making the minimum payment on both each month meant I freed up space to cover the cost of clothes for important events (I had to look the part) and other incidentals, even when a freelance invoice hadn't been paid. I can recall at least one moment standing at a David Jones counter, feigning self-possession as I casually said, 'I'll be splitting this three ways. Here's a Visa, a Mastercard and a debit card.' Then I'd hold my breath until all three cards were approved and a bag with a 'must-have' dress was in my hands. Whatever. I was on the up and it would all sort itself out in the end ... wouldn't it?

In unsurprising news: it didn't. My rising debt burden was a constant creeping darkness that threatened to swallow me. When one of my contracts ended, and I was left struggling to pay for my new lifestyle, I realised I had to return to Melbourne. I needed more affordable rent and a stable existence. I felt like I was admitting defeat. While I'd achieved some great things, I had yet to set up the successful career I'd hoped for.

Attempting serious adulting round two

Back in Melbourne, I got a role writing for the *Melbourne Weekly*, and moved in with a couple in Armadale because the rent was a bargain – about $750 per month. But there were only so many times I could come home after Friday night drinks and feign sobriety while the happy couple watched the footy and sprawled on the couch. I was a third wheel and I preferred to go out rather than hide in my room. The cost of these escapes cancelled out the benefits of the cheap rent.

Next: jackpot. Three months later, I moved into a gorgeous, affordable three-bedroom sharehouse in Brunswick West with my bestie, Beck, and her friend. That was fine for a while, but about six months later, three had become a crowd.

Two grand seemed like a reasonable amount to drop on yet another bond and moving costs. It was normal, and I didn't question it. By this point I was twenty-nine and the amount owing on my credit cards totalled $10,000. But I hoped I'd get things under control as my career progressed. Beck and I threw an '80s-themed housewarming and some killer dinner parties in our Caulfield townhouse. We were inseparable, and we were both finally happy with our living situation. Except for one small problem: our roof was infested with rats. They were having a good ol' time while we slept, and bred faster than they could be removed. The scratching in the ceiling kept us up at night. They'd crept down the walls and were also living between the first and second floors. Occasionally we spotted their shadows scuttling across the terrace, like a flickering black-and-white movie.

A vermin executioner, as I liked to call him, told me the only solution was to move out so that they could cut a hole in the ceiling plaster in order to get to the little buggers above our living room. Naturally, the landlord was not happy with the anticipated cost of this exercise. Presumably, they hoped that the next tenants would be prepared to suck it up. In the meantime, we apparently didn't have grounds to break the lease, so we stayed. After rent, we had just enough of a splurge fund to cover cleanskin wine and the odd takeaway feed. It was frustrating, to say the least. On the surface, we had it all together. But my bank balance painted a different picture. I wanted my home to reflect where I was in my life, so I was paying to live in a decent property, in a nice suburb. But I had limited rights and endless instability.

After months of fighting with the property manager over the ratty and unreasonable conditions, we finally achieved evacuation. It was a bittersweet result though. We had to be out by Christmas Day. Beck and I didn't want to end our time together. But I would be thirty in a matter of weeks. I could barely afford the bond for another place, moving costs would require me to up my credit card limit, and I was already maxed out at $11,000. I could probably squeeze another $2000 out of the bank, but then what?

I had to get my shit together.

My parents, sensing my stress, offered me a spot at their place so I could get back on track. I packed two lots of boxes: one for the room I was moving into at their house, and others that would remain unopened until I'd sorted my life out. I wrapped a porcelain teacup in a page torn from an old issue of *Melbourne Weekly* and sealed my twenties with packing tape.

Failing at adulting

Reality came crashing down around me after the pool party for my thirtieth. My family took me out for a birthday dinner at Donovan's on St Kilda's foreshore. This was a real treat – a special occasion dinner that should have been perfect. But as the sun sank into the bay, so did my hopes. In the middle of the restaurant, halfway through dessert, I sobbed. The waitress asked Mum, 'Is she okay?' Mum smiled and replied, 'She's coming to terms with thirty.' We removed ourselves shortly after my outburst. I woke up the next day swollen with sadness and shame.

I sulked for a week. After calmly enduring my self-pity, Mum served up some tough love: 'You can continue to feel sorry for yourself, or you can start working towards a goal that will help you get ahead.' She was right. I was being a brat. I had to get over myself and start working to undo my mistakes. Although I knew plenty of people my age weren't planning to give up their lifestyles anytime soon, I decided I had to make up for lost time.

In hindsight, I wish I'd had this epiphany much sooner. But I can't change the past and, to be honest, if I had my time over I'd probably do most of it again. It was an adventure and it made me who I am. Your twenties are for experimentation – a time to take risks before settling down. But I could have done a lot of that while stashing away some cash, too. If you're living completely in the now, as I was, or if you're paying too much for your spirited youth, then heed my cautionary tale. In the pages ahead, I share how I turned things around and became a homeowner. I also share the stories of other young people who've forgone brunch, opting instead to plan for a secure future, brick by brick, sometimes in unexpected ways. If I can go from $11,000 worth of debt to owning my own home in a matter of years, it's possible you can too.

A serve of smashed avocado, hold the Salt

In October 2016, well after I'd realised the error of my ways, demographer Bernard Salt penned a column for *The Australian*. 'I have seen young people order smashed avocado with crumbled feta on five-grain toasted bread at $22 a pop and more. I can afford to eat this for lunch because I am middle-aged and have raised my family. But how can young people afford to eat like this?' Salt asked. His piece went viral. And just like that, smashed avocado became the tasty, nutrient-rich dish that defined millennial life.

I was as outraged as my friends. What did Salt know about living in a sharehouse, paying rent and trying to get your career off the ground? Yet, how many times had I paid $30 for brunch when I could have bought a loaf of bread and an avocado for a lot less? Too many to count. Salt's words cut deep, like a knife through a fresh loaf of organic sourdough.

Millennials aren't getting any younger – the generation's elders are pushing forty. According to the Pew Research Center, a millennial is a person born between 1981 and 1996. Also known as Generation Y, many millennials generally came of age around the turn of the century. The internet and smartphones enabled us to live in ways our parents had never imagined – constantly connected and instantly gratified with the tap of a screen, we've been able to get what we want, when we want it. With the exception of housing, that is.

Salt's observations were accurate, but he failed to note that *his* generation, the baby boomers (our parents), bought homes before the most extraordinary property price spike in history. No, it wasn't effortless for them: interest rates were as high as 17 per cent in the late 1980s, compared to the historic lows we're seeing today. But even so, back in 1971, 64 per cent of 30- to 34-year-olds and 50 per cent of 25- to 29-year-olds had purchased a home. Census results in 2016 showed a dramatic decline in home ownership for young people: 50 per cent for 30- to 34-year olds and just 37 per cent for 25- to 29-year-olds.

After Salt's article was published, many commentators countered his arguments. Madeline White wrote in *The Sydney Morning Herald*: 'In my humble sharehouse, we gather, six of us, sometimes more, to chow down on bargain avocado, smashed onto cheap bread, with homemade coffee.' Did your folks ever have to live in a six-person sharehouse? I suspect most didn't. It may have taken them a quarter of a century, but many boomers managed to create relative wealth comparatively easily. They didn't pay for their university degrees and they benefited from many years of a thriving economy.

Of course, most of them went through what I call 'the shit bit' of buying your own home before things got easier. Back in 1984, when I was almost two, my parents bought a modest block of land near the base of the Dandenongs in Melbourne's outer east. In that home I saw them bring both my brothers through the front door for the first time. I rode my BMX along vacant blocks with the neighbourhood kids and mastered roller-skating on the footpath, while Dad hand-paved our driveway. Often we didn't even see Dad during the week because he commuted to the city before we woke and drove home after we went to bed. My folks didn't go out for organic brunches and five-dollar almond-milk lattes when they were my age. They worked tirelessly so we could have a good life. Nothing came easy.

The boomers faced their share of economic challenges, so a bit of empathy between generations wouldn't go astray. Writer Helen Razer made an important point in *Crikey* around the time of Salt's article. While she agreed that millennials faced an income-to-house price ratio that's 'among the shittiest in the world', she also argued that pitting one generation against another isn't helpful. 'Quit pelting cheesy moral balls at each other, and start planning a way out of this awful fondue. We can resume this ancient intergenerational battle when we all have somewhere secure to live,' she wrote.

Is smashed avocado really the problem?

The smashed avocado article stirred up a debate that we should have been having much sooner. It became a national conversation because Salt poked a sleeping bear. A generation had slowly – and silently – been coming to terms with the potential death of the Australian dream. A humble brick home with a Hills Hoist and a barbecue in the backyard – that image at the very heart of our national psyche – had become a fool's aspiration. The boomers had bought them all, pushing prices into the stratosphere in the process. But it's millennials' fault we don't have houses – because we like brunch too much, apparently. Is it any wonder we roared? I had to take all this up with Mr Smashed Avocado himself.

Salt is one of Australia's most respected demographers. In essence, his job is to look at societal changes and predict future cultural trends. Not only did he bring a serve of smashed avocado to the international spotlight, he's also coined the terms 'man drought' (oh yeah, millennial women also have to deal with a bloke shortage) and today he's one of the most in-demand public speakers in the country. There's no doubt that Salt has worked hard throughout his career, but he is also one of the many boomers who've achieved financial success in part by being able to purchase a home before property prices became a sick joke.

Many boomers settled down and bought homes in the 1980s. In 1985, when Madonna's 'Like a Virgin' was a number one hit, you could get a house in Sydney for $88,350 or in Melbourne for $75,200. What a time to be alive. The average weekly earnings were $387.90 – about $20,000 per year – so a Melbourne home was less than four times the annual salary. In the 1990s, property still remained a good investment for Australians. According to the Australian Bureau of Statistics, the average wage in 1995–96 was $28,494 and the median Melbourne house price was approximately $129,000, so houses generally cost 4.5 times an annual salary. In other words, a decade on, the income-to-house price ratio had increased only a small amount.

In a 2017 interview with *Domain*, Salt explains that he and his wife, Kym, bought their Camberwell family home in Melbourne's inner eastern suburbs in 1995. Camberwell has wide, tree-lined streets with a mix of extraordinary Victorian and Edwardian houses. There are Californian bungalows, Art Deco units and modern architectural feats here, too. Properties in elevated streets have uninterrupted views of the city skyline. Back then, a period home in a desirable suburb like this might fetch a remarkable $300,000 to $400,000. According to a land title search, Salt and his wife paid $338,000 for their home. Those who purchased in the mid-1990s got in at the perfect time. Although there was steady growth for two solid decades, the big spike occurred between 1998 to 2003. According to CoreLogic data, capital city property prices increased by a staggering 64 per cent during that time.

Today, trams rattle through the Camberwell junction, while lycra-clad yogis enjoy lattes and brunch, with seemingly little concern about the prices. Developments are going up everywhere. The median house price here is now $2.1 million. Salt says his home needed work when he bought it and it has since been extensively renovated. Pictures show parquetry floors, white walls with large works of modern art, restored fireplaces, a kitchen with flawless stone benchtops and a landscaped garden. But even with the cost of a renovation factored in, a home worth circa $300,000 in 1995 could now be worth more than $3 million. Not a bad result. Even if someone who purchased in 1995 was still paying off a thirty-year loan today, their home equity would far outweigh their debt.

Salt is a difficult man to get hold of. I tracked down his email and made contact several times before he agreed to answer some questions.

I pointed out that there are more factors affecting the millennial generation's ability to buy than a penchant for smashed avocado on toast: HECS debts, stagnant wage growth, and a lack of affordable housing options. But when asked for a holistic solution or a government policy that might help us enter the market, Salt was keen to clarify the point he'd made in his article. 'My initial piece didn't imply that millennials were spending too much on smashed avocado. It parodied the conservatism and moralising of middle-aged baby boomers,' he explained. Okay ... but then he went on to say: 'I think that the house price issue has eased since October 2016 when this story broke. Sydney house prices and even Melbourne house prices have eased since that time, with possibly further to fall. Good news for millennials.'

He's right, property prices did fall. But in the broader context, after a turn-of-the-century boom followed by another fifteen years of price growth, a dip in the market doesn't exactly level the playing field. According to the most recent ABS statistics, the median gross household income is $1616 per week, making the average Australian salary $82,436. The March 2019 *Domain* House Price Report found the median house price in Melbourne was $809,000 – almost ten times the average annual wage. Meanwhile, the Sydney median hovered just above $1,000,000: the average abode in the harbour city costs almost twelve times a typical annual salary. After Salt's story, house prices continued to rise, peaking a year later. According to property research firm CoreLogic, Australian property prices then fell for nine consecutive months to June 2018. Sounds like a dramatic decline, but in real terms house prices dropped a tiny 1.3 per cent. If you were a millennial with a deposit, did this really make a difference? Nope. Not a bit.

By October 2018, property prices had dropped by 4.7 per cent in Melbourne and 7.4 per cent in Sydney. But even after the decline, prices were still 32.4 per cent higher than they had been five years earlier. Prices were down in already inflated markets. Even with the drop, Sydney's median house price only fell $70,000 and Melbourne's $45,000, while prices continued to rise in Brisbane, Adelaide, Canberra and Hobart. It was the blue-chip suburbs in Sydney and Melbourne that were hit the hardest, with some areas experiencing declines of 20 per cent. However, in these cities, where stamp duty has been abolished for first home buyers purchasing at less than $600,000 in Victoria and $650,000 in New South Wales, activity remained strong. More recently, in April 2019, CoreLogic reported that dwelling values had fallen only by a further half a per cent, indicating that the rate of decline was easing. Overall, the national market was down 7.9 per cent from the September 2017 peak. In July 2019, Core Logic reported that prices in Sydney and Melbourne were rising again. Not exactly the crash that had been predicted.

That said, the combination of a softening market and good first-homebuyer incentives does provide a glimmer of hope for millennials trying to enter the market. Of course, that optimism is more likely to infect those who've saved a deposit. For anyone living week-to-week, with little or no savings and just managing the cost of rent, the market still feels miserably impenetrable. For many, stagnant wage growth and the rising cost of living have made it hard to save.

I asked Salt what he'd do if he were a millennial trying to get together a house deposit. Here's what he said: 'I'd create a lifestyle that works from both a saving and a "living" point of view. This means being prudent in saving but it also means "having a life". This might mean it takes a bit longer to get a house, but if property prices are falling, as they are, then waiting isn't such a bad thing.'

Okay, that would be fine if property prices were going to plummet. But with the population increasing, particularly in Sydney and Melbourne, the occasional market correction is unlikely to bring prices back to a truly affordable level. I wonder how Salt might actually manage this mysterious balance between saving and 'having a life'. I suspect he would be chowing down on his smashed avocado while complaining about his HECS debt and the cost of renting like the rest of us.

To be fair, many baby boomers are doing whatever they can to help millennials get into the market. But as Salt points out, this only 'perpetuates social division, with middle-class boomers helping their middle-class kids get into housing. The real issue is how do we create a society where millennials from battler households can legitimately aspire to home ownership in Sydney and Melbourne?' He's not wrong: we are likely to see the gap between rich and poor continue to grow in the coming decades, as some millennials inherit the previous generation's assets, while those doing it tough or who aren't set to inherit, find the market ever-more impenetrable. Even for many middle-class professionals and potential inheritors, the dream already feels out of reach. Salt suggests that while inheritance could help some millennials purchase homes, it will happen much further down the track.

'Millennials will be in their fifties before they inherit their parents' wealth. That's not much help to people trying to build a family in their thirties,' he says.

However, Salt also argues that each generation since the boomers has had lower aspirations of home ownership. 'This is partly because people these days want greater flexibility in terms of travel, work and relationships. Not everyone wants to be tied down to a mortgage for thirty years from the age of twenty-five,' he says. That's definitely true. But what he overlooks is the fact that many people are leading alternative lifestyles to their parents not because they want to, but because there seems to be no other choice.

I asked Salt about the broader societal implications if a large proportion of my generation moves into retirement after renting their whole lives. 'Financial advisers will all say that it is preferable to own your own home before you retire,' he replied. So, what happens if we don't? We know there's a problem with housing affordability, but while politicians are finally taking it seriously and planning to implement new schemes, there are limits to what they can achieve. First-homebuyer grants and other concessions help, but they also keep demand stable, which keeps prices up, so they're a double-edged sword.

It's up to us to drive change. Home ownership is something Australians have always worked hard for. And while we'll work harder than ever for it now, it's not worth giving up on. For me, resetting expectations was key. Property is not something we're entitled to. We can start small, like many of our parents did, and hopefully make incremental leaps over time. If we redefine the dream, it's not necessarily dead.

For first home buyers today, that might mean purchasing an apartment or a regional block, rather than the freestanding suburban home like their parents. It's tempting to blame the boomers for this shrinkage, but while many older Australians will retire with extraordinary property portfolios, plenty won't. I wonder how things will look when we're retiring and our kids are in their thirties or forties. Will the millennials who bought in their twenties and thirties end up with similarly impressive property portfolios? Will we be having the same arguments? Will it be much, much worse?

'Generally, I would say that property is still a good investment in Australia and especially in major cities. As long as this country is growing – rightly or wrongly – there will be increased demand for housing,' Salt concludes.

That's why, if you are in a position to buy, it's important not to be put off by property prices. When you're in your late twenties or your thirties, the bank loves you. You have thirty plus years of employment ahead of you, which makes you a safer bet than older applicants, and the chances are your salary will continue to rise over the course of your career. Property is still one of the best investment options, because not only is it a significant asset, it's a roof over your head.

We can't undo the housing boom, but we can take responsibility for our financial futures. I didn't think my twenties were for saving – they were for living before I settled down. But if I'd been even just a little bit smarter with my money, things could have been different. I'm sharing my story in the hope that you reconsider your lifestyle choices if you're spending like I was. You may not be striving for a house. That's okay. But have a think about where you want to be in the next twenty to thirty years. Are your current spending habits hindering that goal?

Entering the market has become even harder since I started my search back in 2013. Prices have risen further, although in some states they did cool somewhat after I bought. Tighter lending criteria have made it tougher to get the green light for a home loan, but in some places first-homebuyer incentives have improved. The environment people are looking to buy in is constantly changing – but there are other hurdles that most people don't talk about.

Buying a house isn't just about the physical building you get to call your own, it's about living with yourself between those walls. I learnt – the hard way – that it tests not only your relationship with money, but your sense of self. A mortgage might just slap you around until you're a certified adult. There's every chance you'll resent it when it tests you, but you'll love it for pushing you to the edge and beyond.

At no point will I tell you buying a house is easy. It's not. But I do believe it's worth it.

I'll explain how I did it. I'll admit to the risks I took and the mistakes I made. I want you to believe home ownership is possible. Simply realising you're in with a chance if you're prepared to do the work is the first and easiest step. The rewards can be epic. But I want you to go into it with your eyes wide open.

I'll also introduce you to some wonderful people who've thought creatively about what it means to be a modern home owner. In sharing their experiences and principles, I hope it'll get you thinking about a bright future. I've found that although the paths to home ownership vary, they share a three-stage process:

1. Make lifestyle sacrifices and power-save a deposit (or get a leg up from your family).

2. Suffer through the shit bit (there's no way around this – sorry, mates).

3. Come out the other side and realise it was worth it.

The good news is there's more than one way to set yourself up for success.

2

The Power-Save

A FEW WEEKS AFTER MOVING home, and having pulled myself together after my thirtieth birthday meltdown, I sat down with Dad at the dining room table and took a financial whipping. His accounting experience makes him pretty handy with a spreadsheet, budget and projections. I laid all my bank statements on the table. He was appropriately mortified. The taxis, drinks, brunches, clothes, haircuts, travel and spontaneous weekends away had added up to an account balance of precisely nothing. Actually, less than nothing, with the credit card debt.

But Dad looked at my income and said, 'You can almost certainly afford a unit if you save for the next twelve to eighteen months. You can manage mortgage repayments with your salary. They're not much more than the rent you were paying. All you need is a deposit.'

I was stunned, and cautiously excited. I hadn't thought it would be possible on a single salary. I'd been waiting for a guy to come along and work with me to buy a dream home. 'No, Nic,' Dad said. 'You need a financial plan of your own.' I realise the way I'd been thinking was pretty outdated. I'd been fiercely independent in my career, but buying on my own felt like too big a weight. I'd viewed home ownership as something marking the beginning of a partnership, perhaps a family. But what if I followed a different path? And even if I did meet someone, that didn't guarantee financial security.

I was embarrassed that I'd arrived at thirty with no understanding of how to manage money, but I was pretty sure I'd never been taught. I don't remember financial planning ever being part of the school curriculum: weeks of precious teenage years were wasted on Pythagoras's theorem, but the most fundamental mathematics of all, learning how to budget, had weirdly been overlooked. Which is why I'd spent years buying things, looking at the remaining sum in my account and thinking, *yeah, that should do me till pay day.* I believed things would somehow magically come together at some point in the future. How naive.

If I hadn't had Dad, I would have needed to consult a financial adviser or talk to a friend with accounting experience. If you don't have a numbers nerd in your life, I highly recommend getting one. The early financial outlay could help you pocket heaps in the long run. That said, a financial adviser can be expensive – you could be up for thousands if you commit to a full financial plan – money that could go to a deposit instead. However, some banks offer complementary finance consultations, and many financial advisers will give you a first session free. Alternatively, seek out a trusted family member or friend with a finance background. Perhaps offer to buy them lunch in return for some financial tips that apply to your personal situation.

Whoever you get to help you, the first step is appraising where you're spending money unnecessarily. In my case, it wasn't the smashed avocado or even the designer clothes that had done the most damage. It was booze. At a minimum, I'd been buying a couple of bottles of wine a week since I was twenty. If I spent $45 a week on wine, that's

$2340 a year – $23,400 in a decade. And that figure is conservative. I shudder to think about how much money I've wasted in the pursuit of merriness. I drank a deposit and I know I'm not alone. If you spent your twenties living like me, you can't crack the shits about house prices. It was absolutely my fault I didn't own a house yet: I'd spent everything I earned. That's not to say I'd have been able to buy a home where I wanted to live if I'd drunk less, but had I consistently put away $30 or $40 a week from my early twenties onwards, I would have been close to having a deposit on an entry-level investment, instead of having to start from scratch at thirty.

The next step is getting realistic about what you can afford. Dad and I got on Domain and looked at properties in the $300,000 to $350,000 range, which is what we estimated I could handle. At that time, in early 2013, I could get a two-bedroom apartment in a decent block within a twenty-kilometre radius of the city. Looking at pictures of sweet little kitchens and light-filled bedrooms with bright outlooks, I began to imagine what life could be like if I actually pulled this off. Sure, this was more than six years ago and prices rose after this, but in many locations they then started to decline again. Market fluctuations vary from state-to-state and suburb-to-suburb, and first-homebuyer incentives help enormously. So stay with me, friends.

Dad drilled into the numbers in more detail. I was now making about $4000 per month as a social media and content consultant for a public relations agency and in my spare time writing freelance articles that brought in between $500 and $1500 per month. I was often working a six-day week to make this kind of cash, but despite that I was wasting it. 'In a month where you make $5500, you could be putting away between $2500 and $3000,' Dad explained. There were tax requirements that I had to factor in with the freelance income, but when I looked at how much I'd been blowing and what I stood to save, I resolved to knuckle down. All I had to do was give up everything that wasn't essential.

We drew up a power-save plan. I set myself the ambitious goal of saving $25,000 to $30,000 in twelve to fourteen months. I didn't want to live with my parents any longer than I had to. It was going to suck for a year. After that, I'd work out what I could do with whatever I'd saved and return to living like an independent adult. At this point, I still didn't know if $30,000 would be enough for a deposit, but it was a feasible target. When it came time to start seriously researching properties, I'd learn how to use my savings to get a loan.

I'm lucky to work in an industry that lends itself to making extra cash, but there have never been more ways to pocket a quick buck, even if you don't have a degree or formal qualifications. I wouldn't be in the position I am now if I'd lived on a salary alone. Whether you do odd jobs, take on a casual nanny role or drive for Uber, making money in your spare time is the key to getting ahead.

Growing up with property prices that seem impossible to reach has made many of us feel that perhaps we should give up on saving a deposit and enjoy ourselves instead. Study after study shows that we are poorer than previous generations. Rent is astronomical, property prices even higher. We're paying off university debts, and the salaries for entry-level jobs can be laughable. Plus, the gig economy has changed the market – creating more freedom for those who want it, but also reducing security. But, whatever your circumstances are, it's really dangerous to spend everything you're earning. A smart property investment could make money faster than you can. Sure, it probably won't be a little cottage with a bench seat on the front porch, a brightly coloured front door, iceberg roses lining the footpath and a white picket fence, like you – and I – imagined, but it'll be a start, and as the value rises, and the loan is paid down, you can use the equity to take steps towards owning something more desirable.

To get serious about saving, I first had to work out my essential and non-essential expenses. Essentials included car repayments, credit card repayments, phone bills and board. I paid $150 to my parents weekly to cover my share of expenses and my room. At this time, I *didn't* aim to pay off my credit card debt. Dad had suggested it was better to just make the minimum repayments while I saved a deposit. I could deal with the cards once I got into the market. Paying off the cards first would have set me back another year and at that time there was no sign property prices would drop. It was better to get into the market as soon as possible and pay down my consumer debt second.

Non-essential expenses included big nights out, taxis (Uber didn't exist yet), make-up, new clothes, hair and ... brunch. With that, I quit the shops and pricey haircuts. I started searching for bargain cosmetic deals and stopped going out.

That was easy. What I didn't anticipate was the headfuck that came with dialling down my social life.

Many of my friends worked in the media industry. We'd read the articles about the inflated property market. Hell, we'd written some of them ourselves. We'd swallowed the doom and gloom message together. 'Oh, we're poor, might as well go and sink pints at the pub, it's no life without big nights out,' we'd tell each other.

It was bullshit. We were pissing away a fortune on booze, dinners, vices and pointless crap.

Attempting serious adulting (really seriously this time)

When one person says, 'You know what, I'm actually going to start saving,' just watch the friendship dynamic change. It's like when your mate says they're going to stop drinking.

As soon as I started serious saving, this is how conversations about upcoming events would go: 'Nah, I'm going to pass,' I'd say. 'Are you serious? You can't miss this,' my friend would respond.

The problem was this happened *every* week. There was always something I absolutely had to go to. 'You won't meet anyone if you stay home,' my friends insisted. I didn't want to be alone, but if I was really going to reach my power-save target I couldn't go out all the time. Clearly I either needed to get comfortable being on my own or find friends who were prepared to do cheap nights in together. If I continued to go out for $300-plus weekends, I'd be ruined.

The hardest thing about saving isn't the actual saving. If we all agreed to do it together, we'd be loaded. The awful part is having people who aren't ready to do it themselves fight you every step of the way.

When you tell your friends that you're going to stop spending, what you're really saying is, 'I can't be your wingperson when you want to go out.' It's probably going to put pressure on your friendships. When one person in a friendship stops spending so much, the other person might feel vulnerable because it shines a spotlight on their own spending habits. My friends kept asking me to come out for a while. But eventually the text messages stopped.

It's shit. It hurts, and it takes a lot of strength to realise that if people don't support your goals, they're fairweather friends. If they're not there when you start saving, they're absolutely not going to be there when your kid's teething, your partner's driving you up the wall or your mum's seriously ill. Good thing you worked it out now.

I know I could have gone out and said no to the drinks, but I wasn't moving in circles where moderation happened. Ever. Being the sober one is no fun when everyone's spinning around the dance floor and going back to a friend's house to drink more until dawn.

Instead, I got strong. I had a goal I was working towards. That's not to say I never went out. I'd have a drink or two on occasions when I could trust myself to walk away, and I still went to weddings, thirtieths and other organised events. But I wasn't mindlessly dropping hundreds in a single night anymore. There are only so many times you can haul yourself to a cafe after an all-nighter and spend another $50 on a mimosa brunch before you say to yourself, 'Alright, mate, enough.'

So how did my savings plan break down?

I had set myself one year to power-save, so I hustled for maximum income. While the exact amount changed from month to month depending on how much I made freelancing, in an average month I made a total of $4700 after tax.

If you're looking at this number thinking, *that's a lot*, you're right. But no matter how much you make, the principles of saving as much as you can from what you earn remain the same. Work out what you can feasibly save on your income. Be ruthless. Take out all the frivolous spending. Had I been earning less, I would have needed to reduce my spending further. You don't need a takeaway coffee every day, and you don't need to book an Uber when public transport is an option. Maybe you can walk or ride to work. You don't even need a Netflix account.

Look at the cost of your housing. If moving in with your folks is out of the question, is there another way to reduce your costs? A cheaper sharehouse? Renting further out? House-sitting? As unappealing as a step back might be, it doesn't have to be forever.

If you don't think you can save much on your own, find a friend who has the same goal and motivate each other. If you save $1000 each per month, at the end of the year you'll have saved $24,000 between you.

Here's what my monthly spending looked like during the power-save year.

First, I put $2500 per month straight into my savings account. If I did this every month, I'd have $30,000 within a year. But I knew that some months I wouldn't make $4700. Sometimes I'd only make $4000, or I'd have a big bill to cover, so I figured $25,000 was realistic.

After my savings were deposited, I had $2200 left. The essentials totalled $1330:

....

$600 for board and food at my parents' house

$300 for my car repayment

$250 in credit card repayments

$80 phone bill

$100 health insurance

....

That left me $870 to spend – about $170 a week in a five-weekend month, a little more in a shorter month. It was tougher in summer and easier in winter, when going out was less appealing anyway.

I took my lunch to work every day, which meant I didn't spend much during the week. I needed to allow for petrol, the occasional takeaway coffee and skincare products. If that left me with about $100 to spend on the weekend, I'd do something like this: a drink after work ($10), brunch with a friend on either Saturday or Sunday ($25), leaving me $65 to go out on Saturday night. If I'd opted to drop in to a friend's, order a pizza and drink a cheap bottle of wine, I'd have enough left for a cab home. If I did something more affordable, I'd have more for the next weekend. Inevitably I went over budget some weekends, which meant the following week I bought nothing but a takeaway coffee and spent my time writing and watching TV with my parents.

I'll be honest: some months I didn't manage to put away $2500. But when big expenses like car registration hit, and I could only scrape together $2200, I was still on track to reach my target if I recovered the following month.

It was difficult, but there was an upside. I worked out who was on my team and who wasn't. I cemented some of the best friendships I've ever had. My friends Beau and Kim had two small children and would have me over for dinner most Friday nights. We'd cook, drink cheap wine and listen to Fleetwood Mac. I slept on their futon and was often woken by their son on a Saturday morning. He'd poke me in the face and ask, 'Cole, why are you here?' Even in a post-wine haze, I'd smile. For about $25 I could have a great night and wake surrounded by people I loved who supported my goal.

My social life didn't end, it just didn't happen at bars anymore. Those who insisted on having a friendship that took place exclusively in fancy drinking holes were left behind. I need more than rounds of $12 pinot noir to feel valued, but I didn't expect it would take saving for a home to discover who my real friends were.

Delusions of grandeur

Bernard Salt was right about one thing: many of us have set up lifestyles that aren't doing us any favours when it comes to property ownership. A 2018 Roy Morgan study found that millennials were the most likely to be planning a holiday in the following twelve months, with 73.6 per cent indicating they were scheduling a trip, followed by 72.4 per cent of Gen-Xers and 69.2 per cent of boomers.

This may be partly because travel and other lifestyle highs are much easier to save for than homes. You can find bargain return flights to Europe for $1500. But you'll need about $200,000 in the bank if you want to buy a median-priced home in Sydney with a 20 per cent deposit. Is it any wonder we're jetting off to Italy instead of trying to buy in Bondi?

It's not just travel that's preventing us from saving. A 2018 report from the Australian Institute of Health and Welfare showed that a combination of lifestyle choices and a preference for accommodation close to work are limiting the opportunities for young people to move into home ownership. Commuting is shit, and we pay for the privilege of not doing it. In late 2018, the median weekly rent for a unit in Sydney was $550 – in Melbourne, $450 – and many of us are grudgingly paying this, opting for the convenience of living in the inner city over saving a deposit.

Plus, Nielsen research shows that 31 per cent of us have a degree, compared to 19 per cent of our parents, which means almost one in three of us are lugging around a massive university debt too.

Despite the fact that we're putting our money into travel, student loans and rent in pricey suburbs, the Deloitte Millennial Survey 2018 found that more than a third of Australian millennials (39 per cent) believe they will be better off than their parents. Although that's not as high as the global figure of 51 per cent, which includes responses from millennials in thirty-six countries, that's still a good proportion of young Australians with remarkable optimism, despite incredibly high house prices and rising costs of living.

This is nothing short of delusional. There is a long-held belief that each generation will be better off than the last, but statistics show this is no longer going to be the case. A November 2018 report by the Grattan Institute, *Money in Retirement: More than enough*, indicated that by 2056, when Generation Y will be retired or soon retiring, home ownership for people aged over sixty-five will have plummeted from today's 76 per cent to 57 per cent. A handful more than half of us will retire with homes. The rest face renting into retirement. The current retirement system relies on you owning a home. If you don't, you have to cover the cost of living on a pension of $22,000 – potentially less by then – and whatever you managed to put away in superannuation and savings.

Spending on more accessible things that improve our 'you only live once' lifestyle is nothing more than burying our heads in a big vat of freshly smashed avo. In April 2018, research group NPD released data that showed millennials are the 'largest healthy-eating consumer group in Australia', at 32 per cent. But, guess what? Organic and specialist health foods can be seriously pricey. It is possible but difficult to eat well on a budget: our commitment to 'clean' eating might be improving the temple of our body while preventing us from saving for a temple to live in.

We mightn't be buying houses in the same numbers as our folks were at our age, but we're keeping the tourism, hospitality and private rental market thriving. You're welcome, economy.

In doing all of this, we're keeping ourselves out of ownership and jeopardising future financial security. Saving is going to mean some lifestyle sacrifices, but do you really want to keep taking international holidays, eating expensive organic meals and forking out for rent, then limp into retirement with nothing?

If not, get on board, mates. It's time to start accumulating our share of the properties.

Avos of wisdom

 If you're not great with money, get someone to help you set up a budget. This might be a family member with finance experience or a professional financial adviser.

 Don't give up your social life completely but find ways to keep it humble. Seek out mates with shared savings goals to help keep you on track.

 Try to find cheaper rent while you save. Moving back in with the folks isn't an option for everyone. You might be able to live somewhere further out that's more affordable.

 Look at ways to cut back. Eliminate as many non-essential expenses as you can bear. The power-save doesn't last forever.

3

Intergenerational Property Investing

'BYE, AIMEE. I'VE LEFT THE key in the back door,' Aimee Stanton's mother calls from the car before driving away.

'Bye, Mum,' Aimee yells from inside the tiny house she's in the process of constructing.

'We're talking about millennials buying a house and I'm like, "Bye, Mum!" Aimee laughs. She's not your average 25-year-old living with her parents, though. Aimee is a qualified plumber and she's dressed the part: navy shorts, matching navy t-shirt and heavy boots. Her skin is free of make-up and her long blonde hair is pulled up in a messy bun. She tells me people assume she's a hairdresser when she's not rocking her work gear.

Aimee's family provides a perfect example of parents and kids working together, not against each other, accumulating wealth as a team.

Pulling into the family's driveway, there's a house to the left, another to the right and a much bigger residence a bit further up the hill. Her entrepreneurial parents, Peter and Kerry, spent Aimee's childhood buying homes, subdividing blocks and putting a second property on the land before moving on to the next project. As a builder, Peter was able to do this with relative ease.

A decade ago, they settled in Lilydale, in Melbourne's outer east, about an hour from the city. Their historic home, built in the 1800s, overlooks the hills close to the Yarra Valley, a picturesque wine region popular with tourists and wedding parties – meaning consistent short-term rental demand. Melburnians love a weekend away here. Peter built two additional homes on the site, creating easy short-term accommodation for this market and providing extra income for the family.

There's more accommodation in the pipeline, too. In 2018, VicTrack announced it would give away 134 of its retired W-class trams. The family put in an application and successfully secured one for the price of $1000 – all they have to do is pay to relocate it to their land. Later, it will be converted into living quarters.

Inside the partially constructed tiny home, which measures 2.5 by 5 metres, there's a bed frame built into one end and a wall at the other end where the bathroom will be. It is what Aimee hopes will be the first of many tiny homes she knocks together with her dad Peter and thirty-year-old brother Ben, who also lives here. This is the beginning of their property business venture, Tiny Stays. They're in the process of negotiating with nearby landowners to provide land in exchange for a portion of the holiday rental income.

It might sound like Aimee's getting an easy ride, but her path to starting a tiny home business wasn't easy. In 2009, Aimee was failing Year 10. A rebellious student, she showed up for classes at Luther College in Croydon, near her home, mostly just for the social interaction. She spent her weekends binge drinking and struggled with depression. 'I don't know if I was depressed because I was binge drinking, or binge drinking because I was depressed,' she reflects.

But in Year 11, everything changed: Aimee moved to Box Hill Senior Secondary College. 'You are the people you hang around with. The moment I changed the people around me I started kicking goals,' she says, although they weren't quite the right goals at first. Her grades improved, and she signed up for beauty school with some of her friends, but it didn't take long for her to become a beauty school drop-out.

'I did a lot of research. I thought, if I can get a trade under my belt I can go and chase my dream,' she recounts. At that time, her dream was to own a home. She also wanted a pet pig. But Aimee's folks were firm: 'You can't have a pet pig unless you move out and buy a house.' The challenge was accepted.

I follow Aimee through a gate with an archway covered in fragrant mauve wisteria and we step inside an extraordinary home that would sell for millions if it were closer to town. There's a beautiful hallway, a grand timber staircase and a light-filled living room with black-and-white photos of the family hanging on the walls. Lionel Richie's 'Dancing on the Ceiling' is playing in the lounge room, which seems fitting. I'd be dancing on the ceiling too if I'd bought this property ten years ago.

Aimee's dad, Peter, says they stretched themselves financially to secure it. At the time he told his wife, Kerry, 'This is too much, we can't afford it.' But, he recalls, 'I stood on the verandah looking at the garden and thought, 'I can make money out of this.' Indeed, he has.

We sit at a table overlooking the pool and Aimee tells me that at first she was only making $300 per week as a trainee residential roof plumber. This wasn't good enough for a girl who wanted to get into property. A better job was a must. She sent out 100 applications and heard back from one commercial firm willing to give her a shot. It didn't take long for her salary to skyrocket. For a period of time, she was working the day shift and also taking a regular four-hour night shift, too. 'I could earn three grand a week,' she explains. 'But I was still spending a lot of money. I was so materialistic. I had a forty grand car loan. You don't need that.'

Working seventy-hour weeks to save took its toll, but Aimee didn't plan to do it forever. 'I thought, if I work my butt off now, I'll have freedom in the future.' To other people who don't feel like they can save fast enough, she says taking on as much work as possible in the short term is key. 'Sometimes you just have to cop it on the chin and work those hours.'

Soon, Aimee had accumulated enough to buy a three-bedroom weatherboard property with her boyfriend in a pocket of the Yarra Valley called Seville. The couple put in $15,000 each and used lender's mortgage insurance (LMI) to cover the rest of the 20 per cent deposit. Before she'd even turned twenty, Aimee and her carpenter partner had a $316,000 home – and a new pet pig called Crackles.

'People are like, "Oh, wow, you bought a house," and I'm like, "It was only fifteen grand," says Aimee. She believes this is the key to millennials changing their mindset: it's not what the house is priced at that matters; it's what it costs you to get in, before its market value increases and you make money on it.

That's assuming nothing goes wrong. Unfortunately, Aimee woke up one morning and asked herself, 'What am I doing?' A gut feeling that she was too young to settle down descended. Three years after their relationship had started, it came to an end. 'He was a great guy, but I wanted to take a step back and enjoy life while I was young.'

The house had been purchased with the aim of adding to the value. Despite the break-up, Aimee and her ex agreed to finish what they started. Professionally, they were still a perfect match: they could renovate the house using her plumbing skills and his carpentry expertise. all up they spent about $10,000 and sold the house for $416,000 a year after they bought, dividing the profits equally.

'I rocked up to my parents' doorstep with my pet pig and said, "Hey, guys! I'm moving back in."'

Determined not to waste her hard-earned cash, Aimee explored some ways she could invest in property. 'I started looking around at places that I wouldn't particularly want to live, but I could have an investment and it would go up in value,' she says.

While she weighed up her options, Aimee took annual leave from her plumbing job and walked from Melbourne to Canberra. A friend had told her she couldn't do it. Powered by stubbornness, she set out to prove them wrong, sleeping in a tent on the side of the road along the way. 'While I was walking, I had a lot of time to think about what I wanted,' Aimee recalls. The journey was a test of character. One that would ultimately prove just how strong she was on her own and remind her that the best life is one lived, not one weighed down by responsibility. Aimee still wanted to invest in property, but not at the expense of her future happiness.

Along the way, she was sometimes taken in by strangers, but at one point her bag was stolen and she walked for two days in thongs. This would be few people's idea of a good time, but Aimee was experiencing the freedom and exhilaration that she craved. In fact, she enjoyed roughing it so much, she pulled out her phone and filmed an audition for the 2017 season of *Survivor*.

On her return, and after some more research, Aimee settled on investing in Thomastown in Melbourne's north or Frankston in the south-east. She got a mortgage broker to help run the numbers and engaged a property consultant to negotiate prices. This cost her about $5000. 'It's bloody worth it,' Aimee insists. The property consultancy convinced a vendor to sell Aimee a three-bedroom weatherboard home in Thomastown for $416,000, prior to auction. The following week a similar property in the street sold at auction for $100,000 more.

With the loan organised and with a tenant paying off her property, Aimee was free to do whatever the hell she wanted. Which worked out well, because she was selected for *Survivor*: she could quit her job and still pay her mortgage. Sidenote: quitting your job is not necessarily advisable, but Aimee approached it as a calculated risk. With a tenant in her property and enough in the bank to cover any gaps in mortgage repayments, she was set.

Two years later, she hasn't returned to plumbing. Since *Survivor*, despite the fact that she was the fifth evictee, Aimee has built an Instagram profile that enables her to earn cash publishing sponsored posts. 'My fee is $200 bucks for a photo – 'guys, drink this brand of water' she says, holding up a glass and giving the thumbs up as an example. But she's quick to note that she doesn't endorse anything she doesn't like.

Some parents might argue that children should move out when they reach a certain age and learn to fend for themselves. What's Peter's take on this? 'I don't mind helping them out if they don't waste it,' he says. Besides, he gets as much as he gives. 'Aimee and Ben are working smart. They're motivating *me* now.'

'It's not all about money, it's about being happy with my family as well. We're always joking and carrying on,' Peter adds. The strength of the family relationship is the key foundation for their professional arrangement. But is it always fun and games? Ben says that all families running a business together will face challenges, but with a shared vision it works. 'There are some defined roles. We know each other's strengths and weaknesses. We play on that,' he says.

Aimee and Ben are working part-time for their father while they get Tiny Stays up and running. Aimee bounces out of her chair and retrieves a framed photo of her dad from the living room. In it, Peter is wearing a fluoro yellow work shirt and navy pants. There's a Tiny Stays logo and at the bottom it says, 'Congratulations, Peter Stanton, September 2018 Employee of the Month, apprentice carpenter'.

'We called him apprentice carpenter even though he's been a builder for twenty years,' she laughs.

Peter and Kerry have done way more for their kids than letting them move home and helping them with their Tiny Stays venture. They've taught them how to turn their passion into profit. And it's working: they've had 400 applications from people wanting to stay in one of the miniature dwellings.

The tiny home movement has been around since the 1970s, but as housing affordability problems collide with environmental issues, it's really taking hold. Tiny homes can be constructed for as little as $10,000 to $20,000 and can sell for more than $60,000. I ask Ben if they've considered selling their homes to make money faster, but he explains their business model involves 'building them, keeping the asset and renting them'. It means that while the return on investment might be slower, the long-term income stream could be huge. Aimee and Ben moved the completed tiny home to a site in the Yarra Valley in Februrary 2019 and listed it on Airbnb for $179 per night.

But it's been a slow process. The downside of forgoing a traditional salary means Aimee can't access the equity in her home to invest in the business. Most banks require a history of consistent income and savings if you want to refinance your mortgage.

In the meantime, Aimee's also running 'How to Adult' classes at local schools, in the hope that other students don't have to struggle like she did. 'Most people don't realise – they go to uni, get a job and work the rest of their life. There's other ways you can make money and live,' she says.

Why property is an intergenerational issue

You know that kid? The one who insisted they didn't study for the exam, because it's not cool to study for exams, everyone knows that. When asked what they did last night, they tell you they stayed up playing Super Mario Kart until, like, 11 pm. And they look tired, so you believe them. It makes you feel heaps more relaxed about the fact that you didn't study for the exam either. You're pissed when the teacher hands back the exam results a few days later and you see an A+ at the top of theirs. Meanwhile, at least you've somehow managed to pull off a C–. *How did they do it?* You wonder. Well, my friend, they lied to you. They did study.

I reckon there's a similar not-so-funny thing happening in our generation as adults. One minute a couple is renting and the next they're posting a picture on Facebook of an auction board with a sold sign. And we're all like: *how did they do it?*

Just as we didn't like to admit to studying in high school because it wasn't cool, grown-up millennials don't like to admit to getting a leg up into the property market from their folks, because it's not cool. Or fair. Nonetheless, it's quietly happening all around us.

Youth sociologist Julia Cook is part of the team overseeing the Life Patterns project at the University of Melbourne. As part of this longitudinal research, the team has been documenting the lives of a group of millennials since they were in Year 11 in 2005, tracking them at key life stages. Julia is working on her own post-doctoral research project exploring the ways in which millennials are obtaining housing.

Perhaps not everyone wants to be tied down, but for those who are ready to settle in one location there is a very real problem. In 2018, the Life Patterns millennial group was turning thirty. The 2018 findings showed that many of them, especially those ready to marry and start a family, wanted homes in the cities and towns they grew up in. But they're unaffordable. One participant said, 'It is sobering to know that I probably won't have the ability to own my own home or be in the environment that I grew up in.' The researchers have also been following members of Generation X since 1991. When comparing the generations, the researchers found that both groups wanted the same thing at the same age (thirty): to stay in or return to the area where they grew up. But the opportunity to obtain homes where they'd grown up was further out of reach for the millennials. For example, while 80 per cent of the millennial participants were living in the same suburb at twenty-nine as they had been at seventeen, just 11 per cent were living in a house they owned or had a mortgage on. A massive 67 per cent still lived in their family home, while 22 per cent were renting. By contrast, the Gen X participants were almost twice as likely to be living in their own home, within ten kilometres of their family home, by the age of twenty-eight or twenty-nine. In 2017, when she interviewed millennials about their housing situation, Julia found that of those with a mortgage, 'almost 40 per cent had direct financial assistance from family'.

I know what you're thinking. These are the entitled millennials that give the rest of us a bad name. But Julia hasn't found that to be the case at all. In almost all of her interviews, she noted that parents provided some support when it was clear that their child was struggling – when they were seriously considering buying a shithole just to get into the market. It wasn't the kid expecting a handout, it was 'always the parents' offering to provide some sort of help. In many cases, 'it wasn't something that came through in the outset', she says. Which means that parental help came after a deposit had been saved and it was really evident that the young aspiring homebuyer couldn't afford something decent.

The transfer of family wealth from one generation to the next is nothing new, but Julia points to a 2018 University of Queensland study that indicates Australia is one of the few OECD countries that doesn't tax wealth transfers. These were abolished in the early 1980s, which means boomers are not penalised for helping their kids into the market.

But there's an obvious flipside. For millennials without wealthy parents, the barrier to entering the market becomes even higher. 'By trying to elevate, we're exacerbating the problem,' Julia says, explaining that despite the spike in house prices, ownership levels have continued to hover around 70 per cent. She suspects this can be attributed, in part, to transfers of wealth from one generation to the next.

In the coming decades, we could see the gap between rich and poor become cavernous. While some families have worked together to accumulate assets, those who've done it tough will continue to struggle and will face the additional burden of caring for aging parents.

Adult family sharehouses

'Can you bring your washing to the laundry, I'm doing a load of whites,' Mum said.

'Mum, I can do my own washing,' I countered.

'I'm not having the machine on unnecessarily,' she replied, and shooed me off to my room to collect dirty clothes.

People moving home with their parents to save will be subject to relentless digs from those who believe they're getting a free ride. I was seriously grateful for the chance to return home in my thirties, especially because I'd been so stupid with money. But it came with challenges – for all of us. After years of living as I pleased, I felt my wings had been clipped. I lost control and independence. My parents sacrificed space, privacy and their well-earned right to an empty nest. Yet here was this feisty bird-child, squawking about doing things her way.

In the end, I submitted to a 'their house, their rules' approach, which required me to dutifully deliver my whites to the laundry on demand and send a text if I wasn't going to be home for dinner.

Of all the adjustments, losing the space to entertain friends at home was the hardest. I couldn't return the favour when mates cooked for me and I certainly wasn't inviting dates around to canoodle on the couch. No prospective lover wanted to be wedged between my folks watching the late-night news.

Looking back now, I realise my self-esteem took a hit. Forfeiting my independence made me question my self-worth. I couldn't imagine myself as a good partner until I was bringing more to the table. To those who say moving home with your parents is simply an opportunity to bludge, I'd argue that for me it included sacrifice – it induced a social regression. In moving home at thirty, I was actively delaying finding a romantic partnership. But I wanted to achieve financial independence more than I craved love. I hoped it would be worth it.

Apparently, my experience is backed by science. Researcher Jennifer Caputo, from Germany's Max Planck Institute for Demographic Research, has looked into the mental impact on young people returning to live with their parents after a period away. 'Those returning to a parental home after experiencing residential independence report an increase in depressive symptoms relative to their stably independent peers,' the report, published in the American *Society and Mental Health* journal, says.

Yeah. I didn't need an academic study to confirm that.

My parents say they struggled with it at times, too. A family of adults living under one roof inevitably faces disputes, and we had some, but overall I felt I'd come home to a safe haven – a place where I received support on my path to real adulthood. For the first time since I'd moved out, I was in an environment that didn't feel precarious. There was no housemate leaving suddenly and unexpectedly, or the threat of having to move without warning. I didn't have to get used to living with a new stranger. I was protected from spikes in rent and stand-offs about whose turn it was to clean the bathroom. Stability kept me motivated. That and the text messages that said: 'There are leftovers in the fridge if you're going to be home late.'

How can parents help their kids buy a home?

Tom Keel, lecturer in property, construction and real estate at Deakin University says, 'Parents have helped their kids for centuries, passing on the farm, for example. It was once embedded culture – people accepted that was their lot in life.'

'Parents will always want to help their kids,' he adds. However, he acknowledges that as more people fall 'below the line', there's stigma attached to getting into the market with help. And yet he believes that families with the capacity to work together should break down generational silos for mutual benefit, especially because the ageing population threatens to add even more weight to the millennial load.

Parents are going to great lengths to help their offspring build family wealth. They're getting creative about it too. 'Parents are putting the kids' rooms on Airbnb and giving the Airbnb income to them to help financially. I see this in inner-city properties where there are separate entrances,' he says.

But even if you're lucky enough to have parents who can help you buy a home – whether they hand over cash, go guarantor or use equity in their own home – it'll inevitably have an impact on your relationship. Agreeing to work together is only as powerful as the commitment to the plan. Being successful 'involves sacrifices for all in the family', Tom warns. That might mean giving up big weekends or foregoing international holidays so that the nest egg accumulates faster. Tom has watched families stick to a budget and after just two to three years get a deposit together.

But it doesn't work for everyone. 'I also know many parents who won't help their kids after seeing how quickly they spend money when they have it in their hands,' he says.

If you're considering working with your parents to acquire a property, make sure your relationship with your siblings won't take a hit. 'It's very hard to be fair,' Tom admits. That means, if one of you needs help, but two others have entered the market on their own, maybe they deserve some cash, too. For many people, the golden property ticket is off the cards anyway, but Tom says that even small sacrifices made as a family can result in big dividends in the long run. That might start with parents asking: 'Would you like to share a car and put the savings towards a deposit?' It might not be convenient now, but it's going to be a hell of a lot more comfortable than sharing a place with your mum when you're fifty.

If you don't fancy shacking up together, there are alternatives. In 2016, Prime Minister Malcolm Turnbull casually suggested that parents should 'shell out' and buy their kids' homes for them. That's easily done if you're a bazillionaire businessman turned PM, but it's clearly not feasible for the majority of the population. And despite being a member of an apparently entitled generation, I don't know anyone who expects that. If you are debating this with your fam over a Sunday roast, though, here are the options.

Cash gift

Lucky millennials with parents in a position to provide a cash deposit have the opportunity to sidestep the saving process. But keep in mind that you'll still need to be able to prove you can service the mortgage. The bank is going to look at your savings history, what you earn and what you spend each month. In return for the deposit, or even part of it, your folks may look to strike a deal whereby they own a percentage of the property, or of any profits when you sell.

Refinancing the family home

Let's be real, this is a big ask. But if your parents bought a pre-boom home and have been kicking back in their armchairs watching *Gogglebox* while their house appreciates in value, they might be in a position to refinance and put some of that equity into your investment. For example, if they bought their home for $500,000 in 1998 and it's now worth $1.5 million, they've technically made a million bucks. Imagine they still owe $100,000 on the mortgage and they want to take out extra finance on the loan to give you $50,000. The bank says, 'No worries, boomer friends, you've got plenty of equity to borrow against.' So they now owe the bank $150,000, but even if they had to sell at the market value of $1.5 million, they can pay out that loan and walk away with $1.35 million. Your folks might give this to you as a loan that you're expected to pay back so they're not out of pocket. Maybe their contribution is to be returned with interest when you've built up your own equity. The details are up to you guys.

This is a lower-risk option because it doesn't come out of cash savings and you are still completely responsible for your own loan.

A guarantor loan

This is the riskiest option because it relies on you not stuffing up. No pressure! If your parents act as a guarantor, they use their property as security for your mortgage and guarantee some or all of your loan. This means they're taking a risk on their home so that you can get your hands on yours. If for any reason you default on the loan, it becomes their issue. Even if you're the favourite child, they might decide to reduce their risk by securing just part of the mortgage, rather than all of it. If they go guarantor on 20 per cent and you repay that amount later, they're free from responsibility and you're well and truly in the market.

Generally, lenders prefer parents to take out guarantor loans, although some will take applications from relatives. It will help if they have a good credit rating and they're under sixty-five. But even if they're in a good financial position and you are too, unexpected events such as job loss can mean your parents may become responsible for your mortgage until you sort yourself out. Expect family dinners to be pretty tense if your parents are footing the bill for your mortgage as well as their own. If you choose this route, come to a solid agreement for tackling the worst case scenario. Getting a home isn't worth risking your relationship.

*

I know the intergenerational path is not an option for everyone. Unfortunately, there's a growing divide between young people with access to parental support and those without it. Even if you do have parents who can provide some sort of assistance, money issues can complicate the best relationship. That's why there's also a great deal to be said for taking an independent approach – as we'll see in the next chapter.

Avos of wisdom

 It's not your parents' job to get you into the property market, but building wealth as a family can be more effective than going it alone.

 If you're considering it, you need to be prepared for really frank discussions. Make sure your relationship can handle any consequences.

 Remember that even if you have help with a deposit, you still need to be able to demonstrate your ability to save and manage mortgage repayments.

 It can pay to engage a property consultant. Aimee's experience shows that a small upfront investment is worth it in the long run.

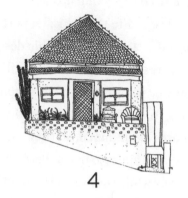

4

You Really Can Do It Yourself

GETTING A DEPOSIT IS ARGUABLY the hardest part of getting into the market. Not all young people have access to help from their folks. Many aren't making a fortune either. But though we might be struggling to save deposits, we've proved we can service high rents and pay bonds. Mortgage repayments on a small unit may be similar to the cost of rent, so your biggest challenge is going to be saving the sum needed to get the loan. The formidable size of that sum isn't stopping determined and creative people from finding ways to save independently: by choosing a lifestyle that costs less, hustling, or seeking out low-income incentives.

Cheaper accommodation can deliver richer lifestyles

In hindsight, I wish I'd thought more about how I could save without making such sacrifices to my lifestyle. It would have been nice to do it like Gary Swift and Rebecca Winther, who've chosen to set up a future while living their best #vanlife.

'We were bored and uninspired by the work, pay bills, work-some-more cycle. We were tired of waking up each day saying to ourselves "There's got to be more to life than this," says thirty-year-old Gary, who works in retail and as a freelance graphic designer.

Bec, thirty-one, works as a labourer. Their skills are ideal for short-term and casual roles that they pick up while simultaneously achieving their dream of seeing Australia. But the best bit: they're not paying rent and their expenses are minimal, so they can actually save while they travel. Genius. Gary's aim is to find a steady stream of online work that he can do remotely while they're on the road.

Prior to stepping out of the rat race, they'd been renting a $330 per week, three-bedroom home in Frankston, in Melbourne's south-east, which wasn't helping them get ahead. So, they moved into a single room in Bec's parents' place. 'Everything we couldn't fit in that small room was sold or donated,' Gary explains. That was the moment they realised how little they needed to be happy. With 'less stuff' they immediately felt freer. For seven months, existing in that tiny space gave them a practice run. If they could handle a cell-sized room, they knew their relation-ship was strong enough to continue if they moved into a box on wheels.

During that time, they purchased and pimped up their van until it was a liveable 'rolling home'. There was only one non-negotiable: it had to be big enough to accommodate Gary's six-foot-four-inch body. Eventually, they settled on a large red 2008 Mercedes-Benz Sprinter, which had ample space for the two of them.

To decorate their home, they had no shortage of Instagram inspi-ration to draw on. Scrolling through bold colour schemes and creative floorplans helped them decide on the look for their tiny digs. They set-tled on a clean white-and-timber mix, with neutral cupboards, small bookshelves and a timber slat ceiling.

'We worked on it straight after work and on our days off, in the rain, the cold and the heat, but it was entirely worth it in the end,' Gary says. In January 2018, they were ready to take off. 'We gave notice to our jobs, said "see ya" to our families and away we went.'

Before they went too far, the couple spent two weeks driving around the nearby Mornington Peninsula as a test run to make sure they had everything they needed. 'Then we went to Tasmania and spent three months down there,' Gary explains. 'It was the perfect place to start living the nomad life, as it's generally less populated and there is an abundance of free campsites.'

Lightbulbs are strung along the walls of the van, and a little blackboard in the kitchen is marked with the words 'the adventure begins'. A stack of pillows and linen have made it a cosy abode. They've added to it as they've gone along, purchasing an awning for outdoor living and entertaining. With backyard views that can be an ocean one day and a stretch of sunburnt country the next, Gary and Bec might just have the sweetest property deal in the country.

They're clever to kick rent to the kerb. It's easily the biggest barrier to saving. Property data firm CoreLogic's September 2018 *Housing Affordability Report* indicated that it now takes an average of 9.1 years to save a 20 per cent deposit. More for a detached home: 9.4 years. If you're in the market for a unit, congratulations, you only have to save for the next 8.3 years. This is hardly a surprise, I know. The report also shows that rents for homes and units currently cost 26.9 per cent of gross household income. How can anyone save when they're pouring almost a third of their income into rent?

The obvious problem with taking that long to save a deposit is the market will likely bolt ahead of even the most diligent saver. By the time you have your 20 per cent deposit, it'll buy you less than what you were aiming for when you started saving. To get a deposit fast, you have to out-save the average Australian. If you don't have a decade to waste, it's time to find dirt-cheap rent somewhere, move home with your folks, or move into a van.

Not only do Gary and Bec cruise wherever they feel like going without losing the roof over their heads, they're also able to save for their own piece of land – whenever they're ready to settle in one spot, that is. Now that they have their miniature home, they can work towards purchasing a vacant block, and they can then continue to live in the van on it until they're ready to build a home.

They're in no hurry though. 'This venture has sort of been like hitting a reset button on our lives. We're hoping to use this time to figure out what we really want, career-wise and personally. Yes, it would be wonderful to be able to live comfortably, but not if it means working 24/7, or in jobs we have zero passion for,' Gary says.

Chasing their dreams is paying off, big time. They've clocked up more than 35,000 followers on Instagram. In between posting scenic snaps, Bec labours and Gary works on freelance design commissions. They're also accepting offers for social media collaborations. 'But we're really aiming to only work with companies that are relevant to our lifestyle and, most importantly, that we genuinely believe in,' Gary says. They recently featured in a tourism advertisement for north-western Victoria, which Gary says was 'an incredible opportunity'. 'Aside from the fun of filming, we got to see this beautiful area that we might not have even considered stopping at on our travels and got to meet and work with some of the locals,' he explains. The couple hope it will inspire more people to live more simply and explore their own backyard.

One of the risks millennials run when they're working to get ahead is curtailing their social life to do so. Gary and Bec have an enviable approach, living and saving simultaneously. By cutting back on the cost of living, they've made more room for inspiration. They recently met a man who lived in a bus and had been travelling for years. 'We got talking to him about life on the road and explained how we missed oven-cooked food,' Gary recalls. 'Next thing we know, he's knocking on the van door with a homemade vegetable pastie for us, fresh from his mini oven.' It's still possible to be generous, even on a strict budget.

To couples considering ditching rent for life in a van, Gary says it can test a relationship. The secret to maintaining peace is to let little grievances go. 'There's no space to hold grudges in a van.' They also make a point of regularly doing things separately, even if it means going for a walk while the other person stays in the van and watches a movie.

The advantage of checking out Australia while rumbling along in their trusty van is they get to road-test a heap of potential regions and lifestyles. 'We haven't seen enough of the country yet to know for sure where we'll settle down,' Gary says. He really loves the idea of setting up in Tasmania. 'Bec's more of a warm-weather girl and really liked the Noosa region and the townships of Agnes Water and Seventeen Seventy,' he adds. 'We might have to find a compromise somewhere in the middle.'

Saving while renting

Of course, most people's circumstances don't allow for packing up and embarking on a nomadic adventure, so how can you save if that's not an option? Most young professionals need to rent, often reasonably close to work.

Take Laura, now thirty, whose rental journey started at the age of twenty-one. While studying arts and science at Melbourne University, Laura lived in a range of sharehouses – a warehouse conversion in Brunswick, and a 'dodgy terrace' in North Melbourne. She also completed two exchange programs: one in Hong Kong and another in Montreal. After meeting her boyfriend, Myles, who's also now thirty, at uni, she later moved into his Carlton sharehouse. By this point Laura was twenty-five. 'There were nine people,' Laura says. Three sets of couples and three singles. 'That was my last crazy sharehouse,' she laughs. After that, they moved into a quieter sharehouse in East Brunswick.

At that stage it made little sense to get their own place and they enjoyed the social aspect of sharehousing. As early-career geologists, Laura and Myles were often on exploration trips for weeks at a time. Myles would journey to Western Australia and Laura was frequently in South Australia or the Northern Territory. 'Sometimes our stints away wouldn't line up and we wouldn't see each other for a month,' Laura says. The upside was they were both paid to camp in the outback. There's nothing to spend money on when you're in a remote location looking at rocks. So, they committed to saving as much as possible. 'When you're not a student anymore, it's getting real,' Laura says.

In January 2016, the saving mission got serious. A mate with a sharehouse in Northcote suggested they get a caravan and move into his backyard. They forked out $2200 for the caravan, purchased from a surfer. 'It took eight friends to help lift it in,' Laura recalls. The couple painted their temporary home and moved in, paying approximately $100 per week to contribute to the sharehouse and access the kitchen and bathroom. 'It was the most fun time of my life,' Laura says. They lived there for four months, before moving into a room in the sharehouse when winter came.

By December 2016, when Laura and Myles were twenty-seven, they'd saved a 20 per cent deposit for a property. With a maximum budget of $340,000, Laura headed to the auction while Myles was away. It was a two-bedroom unit in Reservoir, about 12 kilometres from Melbourne's CBD. 'I stood by myself at the front trying to look as confident as possible,' Laura explains. She secured it for $336,000. It all felt a bit surreal. She remembers thinking, 'Is this how you buy a house? Great!'

Once they were in their home, their mortgage repayments were $290 per week – not much more than they'd paid in their East Brunswick and Northcote sharehouses, so they continued to save just as they had before. By 2018, with additional savings and equity in their unit, they bought a three-bedroom house in Preston, which they've rented to friends for $460 per week, while they remain in Reservoir. The plan is to eventually move into the Preston home. Laura continues to travel for work, while Myles is now working on the Melbourne Metro Rail Project. 'At least Myles is here now ... underneath Swanston Street,' she says.

In case you're wondering, the caravan remains in the backyard of the Northcote sharehouse, where it has become a hub for their friends. 'People have been in and out. When someone needs a break or friends need somewhere to stay, it's there. It's so lovely to still feel connected to that community.'

The struggle is real

Laura and Myles worked hard, but they also had the benefit of being a dual-income couple. Is buying totally out of the question if you're a single person on a low income? Not necessarily. It's worth investigating the government incentives in your state to see how these can help to reduce the amount you need to save. First-homebuyer stamp duty reductions and exemptions in some states have made a huge difference.

In Western Australia, the state government has invested heavily in Keystart Home Loans, which enables single people earning less than $90,000 and couples earning a combined income of less than $115,000 to apply for a loan when they have a deposit of just 2 per cent. In Victoria, the HomesVic Shared Equity Initiative pilot program launched in 2018, to help up to 400 low- to middle-income earners buy a home with a deposit of 5 per cent. By March 2019, more than 150 homes had been settled. The government provides up to 25 per cent of the price and therefore has a 'proportional beneficial interest', which means that, if you sell, the government's contribution must be paid out.

Here's an example of how the HomesVic scheme works. If you earn $65,000 and want to buy a $460,000 home, you'd usually need a 20 per cent deposit of $92,000. However, under this scheme, HomesVic could invest 25 per cent – $115,000 – while you pay a 5 per cent deposit of $23,000. This also means the loan comes down to $322,000, in turn bringing your mortgage repayments down to approximately $1600 per month – less than they would have been if you'd applied with a smaller deposit. If, over time, the value of your property rises, you may choose to refinance the loan to return the government's portion. Once you've paid off the government's proportional beneficial interest, it gets reinvested into other homes.

Toughing it out

Not everyone can hustle to pull a deposit together fast. For some, saving will take years. It's the dedication to the outcome that will get you through. Few people know this better than Ana Tuckerman. Ana's a single parent to nine-year-old son EJ and has consistently lived on a strict budget to make her home-ownership dream a reality. At forty-six, it's taken her more than half a decade since she started saving.

Previously, Ana, a school teacher, was renting in Melbourne's inner-west suburb of Yarraville, spending $1900 per month. She often read articles about older women without homes being susceptible to homelessness, and she was determined to avoid becoming a statistic. Ana's accustomed to living with very little. When her son was born in 2010, she lived on paid maternity leave for twelve weeks, and then on single parenting benefits of $700 per week plus family tax benefits. She also received a baby bonus, which covered the cost of a pram, car rego and health insurance for the year. She had a small sum for emergencies, but purchasing a home seemed unfathomable at that time.

In 2014, when EJ was four, Ana chose to take a voluntary redundancy – a risk to her stable income, but an opportunity to receive a lump sum of $18,000, which would have taken ages to save. She promised herself she wouldn't touch the payout, and went on to work as a sessional university lecturer. This paid inconsistently – from December to February there was no work – but Ana always budgeted to ensure she was adding to her house-deposit funds. She kept a calendar with all dates for payments marked so she was aware of exactly what her position was at all times. 'I paid myself a living wage. I worked out what I needed for food and incidentals, bills, saving, then myself and my son,' she explains. 'There were times when I could only put $25 a week into savings, and times I could put $250 in.' After bills and saving for a depost was accounted for, Ana left herself $280 per week. 'That was food for my son and I, petrol, and my Myki card. If that went, I had nothing.' So it was difficult to save, but in that three-year period Ana still put away about $10,000.

By the time EJ was in Grade 1, Ana was in a position to return to full-time teaching, which provided a stable income and made her a reliable prospect as a home loan applicant. But even then, Ana remained on her frugal budget, getting a haircut just once a year and rarely buying new clothes. Ana got pre-approval for a home loan of $400,000, which included lender's mortgage insurance (which I'll discuss in Chapter 8), as she didn't have a 20 per cent deposit. She looked for a year around the inner-western suburbs of Melbourne, such as Footscray, but kept losing to bidders who offered $410,000 or more for small units. Ana could have looked further out, but her mothers' group was an integral part of her community and she was reluctant to uproot herself or relocate EJ. 'I was prepared to live in a one-bedroom with my son; at least I'd be in the market.'

After finding out about the HomesVic incentive, Ana discovered it would potentially allow her to get something bigger where she wanted to live. Her application was successful and she received a contribution of $114,400, in addition to her own 5 per cent deposit ($27,600). This gave her a total budget of $552,000. In September 2018, she bought a two-bedroom unit in West Footscray. The large deposit brought her mortgage down to $410,000, and her repayments are approximately $2000 per month – similar to what her rent in Yarraville had been. Now Ana and EJ have a small garden, the garage has been turned into a playroom, and, to EJ's delight, they have a cat.

Ana is giving herself a well deserved 'year off', a breather from years of living strictly. She'll start saving again in 2020, with the aim of paying out some of the HomesVic contribution. In the long term, she'll see if she can use equity in the property so that she can take on the loan independently. But for now she's content to enjoy her home. 'In my thirties, I thought I would never own a house. I just couldn't see how I could do it.' But there's nothing like caring for a small child to realise just how capable you are. 'I needed that security for my son and myself,' Ana concludes.

Avos of wisdom

 Consider creative ways to reduce your rent and living expenses without giving up the aspects of your lifestyle that you value the most. Cut the rest, and remember, the deposit power-save doesn't last forever.

 Find out what government incentives apply in your state and whether you're eligible for them.

 Think about how strict a financial diet you would be prepared to adopt if it meant you could buy a house within a couple of years.

5

The Rise
of Rentvesting

THE TERM 'RENTVESTING' WAS COINED to describe the trend of buying in a more affordable suburb while continuing to rent in a more desirable one (for instance one closer to work). When I picture a rentvestor, I imagine a savvy young thing with Instagramable style, who's casually dropped some coin on a sweet little pad that's going to spike in value, without having to forgo the lifestyle they've created for a second.

Growing up, it never occurred to me that I wouldn't be able to afford a home with a garden and a picket fence. Reality started to set in with every sharehouse move and rental hike. I've worked hard since I was a teenager. Even if I hadn't pissed away my twenties in a whirl of booze, clothes and travel, buying a freestanding home (rather than a unit) would be a struggle. Only the very wealthy can buy a large home in a big city as their first home these days. For the rest of us, the dream has changed and we have to get creative.

If baby boomers were known for following a well-worn path – get a job, buy a home, have a family – millennials will be known for taking countless paths that not only enable them to get ahead, but also enjoy lifestyles that reflect their values and aspirations. In 2018, *Vice* conducted a survey of more than 7000 millennials and found 85 per cent of us wanted to own homes. Only 6 per cent didn't. But 48 per cent said they'd rather rent for longer to be closer to the conveniences they needed. For those people, rentvesting might be the solution. You buy a small property investment, without giving up everything.

Some of us are delaying home ownership and starting a family, with the average age of marriage for men 31.9 and for women 29.9, well up from the 1974 averages of 23.3 and 20.9 respectively. We're also far more entrepreneurial than our folks. Unlike previous generations, our paths to home ownership and financial freedom will be as unique as our career choices.

I began to think about my property as an investment rather than a home, which meant I had to make decisions with my head instead of getting too emotionally attached. Difficult, seeing as I get emotional about $300 dresses. How could I avoid getting attached to something that was going to cost me more than $300,000?

Easily, it turns out. Instead of getting caught up in the building itself, I got acquainted with the concept of 'rentvestor'. My goal was to buy smart, live in my investment for twelve months and then rent a place I loved where I wanted to live. Living in the property I bought for the first twelve months would mean I was eligible for first-homebuyer benefits, such as a reduction in stamp duty, which would reduce my upfront costs.

I figured the upside of not being able to afford my dream home was that I didn't have to be bound to a mortgage for thirty years. Of course, the mortgage would be there, but with a tenant to pay it off, I could do what I wanted. Once I'd decided to become a rentvestor, I knew that for a couple of years life would be hard. After a tough period of saving, I would have to start paying off a mortgage by myself and live in an unfamiliar suburb. My lifestyle was going to suck for the foreseeable future: crunching the numbers, I'd have to live frugally to make ends meet. But hopefully the churn would have an end date and I could then cobble together a life like the one I'd enjoyed before – but with improved spending and saving habits firmly in place, and an investment for my future.

Is rentvesting a good idea?

Some experts will tell you it's preferable to purchase a home to live in, rather than an investment. I, like many millennials, simply couldn't afford to save a deposit for a home where I wanted to live. The aim was to take my first step onto the property ladder and have a long-term investment that would build equity over time and perhaps, down the line, use that as leverage to buy something else.

This strategy wasn't without risks. For an investment property to be a good move, you rely on it going up in value over time. During the housing boom, that might have been up to 4 or 5 per cent each year. In the next few years it could be less, but even so, the hope is that it will appreciate in the long term. I knew I would have to allow for market ebbs and flows. I understood the value might rise, drop off for a while and then hopefully rise again.

This might sound obvious, but the aim is to get a tenant who pays rent covering all, or almost all, of the mortgage, minimising your out-of-pocket costs. The key is to choose an area with high rental demand. With the mortgage covered, you can rent where you like while your investment gets paid off.

What is equity?

Home equity is the difference between the market value of your property and the amount you owe. In simple terms, if you purchase a property worth $350,000 using a 20 per cent deposit, your loan might be $280,000, which means you have up to $75,000 in equity. Banks allow you to borrow against this equity. If, over time, you pay your loan down to $250,000 and the value of your property rises to $500,000, you have approximately $250,000 in equity. Having said that, you might not be able to borrow against all of it. Many banks will set a percentage of the property's value that you can borrow against – 80 per cent, for example.

Equity becomes like an asset itself and allows you to do a number of things. You could use your equity to do some home improvements to add value to your property. Or you could use it to purchase your next investment: instead of saving another deposit, you borrow against your equity to secure your next place. You can also use your equity as a personal loan – you might buy a new car or take a holiday, but ideally you want to use your equity to build more wealth.

It's not something you necessarily want to do straight away – borrow against your investment – even if you have equity soon after purchase. If the value of the property drops to $250,000 and that's the amount you owe, you have no equity. In this case, you'll need to ensure your repayments are made while the market is in a slump, because if you can't maintain the mortgage, you'll need to sell and hope you achieve a price in line with what you owe. In the worst case, if you sell it for less than you owe, you're liable for the difference. You really don't want to have to sell at a time like this. You're better off finding a way to make the repayments and holding onto the investment until it's in a position to pay you a return.

The way you use equity is up to you. During the boom, many people used equity to build their investment portfolio fast. But if you use equity to purchase a second investment and for some reason the values of both your properties drop, there's a risk of winding up with negative equity. That's where your properties are worth less than you owe.

Property investment is not a get-rich-quick scheme. If you want it to pay dividends, you need to be in it for the long-haul. As long as I have a reliable tenant in my property making rental payments on time, allowing me to pay my mortgage on time, market fluctuations don't worry me. Later, I'll tell you more about how I used my equity. It took a few years before that was an option.

How can a buyers agent help you choose the right property?

A buyers agent, or buyers advocate, represents you, the buyer. This is important because an agent selling a home is working for the vendor, the seller. 'A buyers agent levels the playing field – both sides have professional representation,' explains buyers agent Kate Vines.

A buyers agent may seem like an unnecessary additional expense when you're on a budget, but if they're able to save you thousands, working hard to negotiate the right price or preventing you from paying too much at auction, they can be a valuable investment. Fees will vary from firm to firm. 'An engagement fee might be circa $1000,' Kate says. In most cases, you won't be charged again until you purchase. The total cost of engaging a buyers agent might be $10,000 – but it could be more or less, depending on the level of engagement. For example, you might simply engage them to help you find the right property, and then terminate their services. Alternatively, they can provide the full package, assisting you right through until settlement. Many will expect to be paid shortly after the purchase contract is signed, but you may be able to negotiate alternative arrangements.

At the very least, a buyers agent can bid on your behalf at auction. Kate charges approximately $500 (+ GST) to bid on a buyer's behalf and another $500 if they're the winning bidder. That can be $1000 well spent if you win a stressful auction because you've got a cool-headed expert putting their hand up for you.

Like anything, you get what you pay for. Be cautious of those who charge a low flat fee – they'll be trying to get you to buy something quickly to make a transaction, so they get paid,' Kate says. It's also worth quizzing any prospective buyers agent to make sure they're truly independent. Some might have existing relationships with particular agencies or developers who offer them financial incentives if they can sell their properties to clients. Kate has advice to make the right choice: 'Take them up on the free consultation. I meet with people cost-free. They'll make a decision based on my authenticity.'

A good buyers agent will work tirelessly to help you find a property that really does meet your budget and lifestyle needs. That said, Kate also encourages her clients to do their own searching, too. 'The one thing I cannot do is tap into your emotions,' she points out.

But the most important thing a buyers agent can do is use industry knowledge and experience to get you the best possible price. Kate highlights a property she bought for a client in April 2017. The two-bedroom apartment in the Melbourne suburb of Hawthorn East was secured for $517,000. Kate knew the agent wanted to get the deal done fast and as a result was able to negotiate a competitive price. Six months later, another unit in the same block sold for $595,000.

She's quick to explain that not every sale will be a bargain, but it should be in line with market expectations. Once Kate's been engaged she rarely fails to find a property for her client. 'Over the course of the process, we'll have many discussions and I'll be honest with them if their expectations are unrealistic for their budget. Typically, this disconnect is the reason a person can't find a property,' Kate says. When this happens, it's her job to educate her client and help to explore alternatives.

If you're not going to use a buyers agent, it's essential to know the market inside out. Kate suggests looking for at least six months before buying. This gives you a chance to go to a range of open-for-inspections and auctions. 'Keep every brochure, write notes about how many bidders there were. Three, six or no bidders? Did it pass in?' Looking at the results on the internet won't paint a clear enough picture, she explains. The more information you have about market activity in the suburbs you're looking at, the better placed you'll be to negotiate the right price.

How to choose a suburb that's a good investment

Buyers agent Matt Skehan knows how to choose a suburb to invest in, and he hasn't restricted himself to his home town. The 33-year-old started developing an interest in property back in 2009, when he was working as a physiotherapist, running his own business. He had the opportunity to buy a place, but the bank wouldn't give the green light. 'As a self-employed person it was hard to get finance,' he recalls.

This turned out to be a blessing in disguise. While he continued to save, Matt improved his position and taught himself about investment strategies. When he was eventually in a position to buy in 2011, having saved a deposit and improved his business's cashflow, he bought a two-bedroom ground-floor apartment with a courtyard in the beachside Melbourne suburb of Elwood. The 1930s Art Deco property was one in a block of just four, moments from the beach.

This rare find fitted the bill as an investment. Matt was looking for scarcity and there's only a handful of small Art Deco apartment blocks in Melbourne's inner bayside suburbs. They retain their value because they have historic significance and character. 'Supply is the enemy of capital growth,' Matt says, and explains that limited stock is what aspiring rentvestors should look for when choosing a suburb to invest in. He'd found a 'diamond' and believed that quick capital growth would enable him to take his next step and buy a second investment on the back of it.

By 2013 he was in a position to buy again. This time he looked to Sydney, where the rental yield is strong – much higher than in

Melbourne. He bought a property in Randwick, six kilometres from the city.

Rent yield is the amount of rent you make annually, divided by the property's price. For example, if you paid $350,000 for your property and make $300 per week in rent, you're bringing in $15,600 per year. That makes your yield 4.46 per cent.

'Yield is important for your cashflow, because when your yield is low, it reduces the income your property brings in,' Matt explains. 'I went interstate at that time because I was looking at yields. Sydney was prime for growth after a period of underperformance.' In terms of yield, 'Melbourne wasn't as attractive' at that time. Sydney is surrounded by a harbour and mountains that restrict its potential for urban sprawl. Without the potential for growth that exists in other cities, Sydney remains a valuable long-term investment, despite the higher prices.

Today, Matt and his wife have six properties. And yes, despite this impressive portfolio, they're still renting in the Melbourne bayside suburb of Sandringham. 'The areas we want to live in are quite expensive; it's easier to build up some equity,' he says.

Being rentvestors has given the couple the freedom to rent a good home in an affluent suburb, without having to buy there. Now that they have a two-year-old, they'd eventually like to buy a family home – selling one or two of their investments down the track will enable them to do that.

Matt developed such a strong passion for property investment that he decided to ditch physio to become a buyers agent in 2017. He now helps people all over the country get into the market. Many of his millennial clients are rentvestors. A young couple renting in Cronulla, who've bought a property in Melbourne because they couldn't afford Sydney, are a good example.

When you're looking for the right suburb, Matt reckons it's a good idea to cast your net wide. What you need to look for is a suburb with 'lifestyle drivers', such as a beach or cafes. 'An area that has been daggy but has lifestyle drivers' is a smart bet, he recommends. You personally may not want to live there, but it should be desirable to prospective tenants.

Many experts will tell you that being close to transport is essential, but Matt says this depends on where you buy. In Melbourne, for example, traffic is thick and public transport is essential, while in Adelaide, it's not absolutely necessary, because with a population of 1.3 million it's a '25-minute city': you can easily get anywhere in the car within half an hour.

'I'm a big fan of walkability,' he adds, reeling off other cities including Geelong in Victoria, Brisbane and Adelaide, where he's bought places for clients who are able to walk to shops, schools and transport.

Every city has different lifestyle drivers. In Brisbane he highlights 'river suburbs' such as New Farm, which will continue to retain desirability as the city grows. Brissie residents are reliant on buses, but being two kilometres from the city, New Farm will remain an attractive prospect regardless of the infrastructure that develops in Brisbane's suburbs over time.

While it's worth exploring a range of suburbs, once you've settled on one it's time to get specific about the qualities of the street. Matt tells his rentvestor clients to get granular: a 'wider, tree-lined street with period homes' is going to impress your future tenants far more than a dark little alleyway. The streetscapes change dramatically from suburb to suburb, so you need to get hyper-local when choosing the right investment: making a list of the appealing qualities of one spot over another can quickly make is clear which is a better bet.

Proximity to schools is a bonus, but Matt says this is 'not the be all and end all'. In Melbourne, he says, clients who buy in the zone for a selective school will pay a premium – sometimes 10 to 15 per cent more than surrounding suburbs. McKinnon Secondary College in Melbourne's south-east is a selective school that requires people to live in the catchment zone, and that pushes property prices up – but there's no point in buying there if you're paying a premium you actually can't afford.

That's a pretty non-negotiable bottom line. 'You've got a budget. If you're an investor, ultimately you're directed by how much money you have,' Matt points out. It's more important to look at how the city you're investing in is growing. While it might be tempting to look in 'greenfield sites' – areas marked out for potential new house and land development, often on city fringes – you have to, again, consider scarcity. If you're buying in a spot with plentiful house and land offerings, then your purchase isn't scarce, so your capital growth isn't likely to be rapid.

How to avoid screwing up an investment

For me, investing in property was about buying something that would hopefully go up in value over time, but also something that at any point could be a roof over my head if I needed it. That's why I chose to rule out investing in another state. Instead of buying property, I *could* have invested in shares or stashed my cash in a high-interest account and relied on compound interest. But you can't sleep in shares and a bunch of numbers in your bank account won't keep you warm at night. This is why property was my first priority. In time, I did hope I'd also be able to do those things: buy shares and gain interest on accumulated cash in the bank. But first, a property would be an investment that I could live in, both for the first twelve months and at any time life demanded it in the future.

Buying an investment property comes with an inherent risk: that you may one day not be able to make mortgage repayments. If the market crashes and the value of the property falls below what I owe, I still have to pay back the difference, so my priority is making sure repayments are made consistently. Although my plan was ultimately to get a tenant, I could always become the tenant if for some reason I couldn't find one. I'd be paying what I'd pay in rent elsewhere anyway. If my circumstances changed, my investment could again become my 'home', which is why I didn't want to buy something so far away that I couldn't possibly move back in.

The opportunity outweighed the risk: the value of a well-considered investment could rise much faster than I could possibly save. The aim was to ensure that from month to month it wasn't costing me much more than I would have paid in rent anyway. I had to buy where people needed to rent, and that rent had to be enough to cover the mortgage repayments. My long-term goal was to convert that investment into a home I lived in – moving back into it in the future, or, even better, using the equity I'd accrued to get somewhere bigger and better down the track.

I had identified the qualities that would help me find the right property for me. For my investment to be a good buy it needed:

- to be in a suburb with a reasonably strong rental market, so I could find a quality tenant relatively easily

- to be in an area with growing demand, so that hopefully the value would rise and it would build equity, which I could use later to buy something else

- to be far enough away from the inner city to be affordable, but not so far that I couldn't live in it if I needed to at some point

- to have a price tag that made the mortgage repayments achievable – ideally not too much more than I had been paying in rent.

Working out what you can borrow

It took a while for me to get my head around what I could – and, more importantly, *should* – borrow. Like, is it better to take the maximum amount the bank would give me? And how do they decide how much debt I can take on? What impact would the amount I borrowed have on my monthly repayments?

An online mortgage calculator is a good start when you're trying to understand how the numbers stack up. Most banks' websites have them. There are calculators to help you work out your borrowing capacity, mortgage repayments, stamp duty and equity. Start by getting an idea of what the bank might give you based on your circumstances. You'll plug in the number of people applying for the loan, the number of dependants, your income, monthly expenses and credit card debt. You'll also choose whether it's your home or an investment, as well as whether you're a first home buyer.

In recent years, banks have become increasingly conservative when assessing borrowing capacity. This is partly because they got a bit trigger-happy and started handing out loans to people who couldn't necessarily afford them. Now, the bank will review your application based not on what mortgage rates are today, but on what they could possibly rise to in coming years – their strategy to ensure you can afford interest rate hikes if they happen. In June 2019, the Reserve Bank cut cash interest rates to 1.25 per cent – a record low. Banks are generally encouraged to pass the cut on. Home-loan interest rates are a little higher than cash interest rates and each bank's rates are at their discretion, hovering anywhere between 3 and 5 per cent, depending on the loan type. Even if your lender's interest rates are at 4 per cent, the bank might review your position based on an interest rate of 7.25 per cent. This protects the banks from granting a risky loan, but, as mortgage broker Ben Ong says, it also protects you from falling into a position where interest rates rise and you can't afford repayments.

'If your mortgage is $300,000 at 4 per cent interest, you're going to pay $12,000 a year in interest,' he explains. But if interest rates go up to 7.25 per cent, that amount increases to $21,000. When the bank considers your circumstances, they want to ensure you could cover that extra $11,000 if you had to.

Ben says banks are also taking a closer look at people's monthly expenses and ongoing costs – another reason to cut down on buying things you don't need while you're saving a deposit. When they review your bank statements, the bank will see you're good at living on the cheap. If you're planning to buy as an investment, they'll also factor in things like council rates and the cost of a real estate agent managing your property – that could be anywhere between 5 and 10 per cent of your monthly rental income, depending on location and your chosen agent.

Another key thing: they're also going to consider the type and location of your dwelling. 'Apartments, and in particular high-rise or small apartments, are the biggest cause for concern,' Ben explains. He says banks have 'postcode lists' and those places on the list are harder to purchase because there might be a housing oversupply. He points to suburbs like South Yarra in Melbourne, where there's a stack of high-rise developments. To get loans for such areas the banks might 'want bigger deposits, particularly for investment purchases'. Prospective rentvestors looking to buy apartments need to consider suburbs where there aren't too many developments or rental vacancies, unless they're prepared to put down more than 20 per cent.

Some regional locations might also require a bigger deposit if banks deem them risky. But that's not the case across the board. 'Regional Victoria and NSW property prices are actually outperforming capital cities over the last year or so, because of people looking for the elusive foot in the market,' Ben says. 'But there are only so many people that can either make the appropriate income away from a jobs hub or make the commute.' If you're considering a regional investment, look at areas with a realistic commute. Something further out might be cheaper, but if it doesn't meet the bank's lending criteria you may struggle to get a loan.

Our parents looked for homes they could live in. But Ben points out that millennials are living different lives to their folks. Rentvesting provides the flexibility to move as our lives evolve. Rather than locking in a thirty-year mortgage and planning to live in the one home for three decades, rentvestors will often view their investment as a ten-year stepping stone. Yes, you still get the thirty-year mortgage, but rentvesting enables you to re-assess and potentially change things up as you move through life stages.

All the single ladies

To understand the growing appeal of rentvesting – and why it might be suitable for you – Ben says it's useful to consider the cultural influences on the property industry, not just the numbers. Population growth and the Australian appetite for home ownership are key factors in the solid two-decade rise in property prices, but what's often overlooked, he says, is the increased buying power of women.

It's pretty hard to believe that it took until the 1990s for dual-income families to become the norm. 'When I was a kid most of the households were single income,' Ben, who's thirty-seven, recalls. Today, not only are women matching the purchasing power of blokes, in some cases they're outperforming them. 'In a lot of households, the female's working, she's getting a share of the income or she's the primary income driver,' Ben points out. This has a huge impact on household wealth. It means that young families may be in a position to purchase a small investment while renting a place that accommodates the family elsewhere, even if they can't afford the large home on a big block.

Healthier household incomes are backed by a ravenous hunger to enter the market. Westpac's 2017 Home Ownership Report showed that 22 per cent of women were considering buying an investment property in the next five years, compared to 11 per cent of men. This is reinforced by ABS data. In 2015–16 more women (60 per cent) lived in a home they owned or bought than men (56 per cent). In addition, young women were more likely to buy a property than men: 26 per cent of women aged fifteen to thirty-five had a mortgage, compared to 20 per cent of men in that age demographic.

For some women, shacking up with a partner is no longer a financial imperative. This is partly why we'll continue to see more women investing, and rentvesting, independently. The trend is backed by ABS figures that suggest there'll be a spike in single-person households in coming decades, rising from 2.1 million lone habitants in 2011 to a projected 3.4 million in 2036. So, whether you're living in a one-bedroom place yourself or renting a small investment to someone else, it's likely there's going to be a market.

Mind you, it still pays to pool your resources if you're in a partnership. Ben explains that two people making $100,000 each are better off than a single person earning $200,000. Why? The couple has two tax-free thresholds and therefore a lower tax rate. The person on $200,000 is losing 40 cents in every dollar, so the couple has a net benefit of $15,000 to $20,000.

An eye on the future

'What will your position look like in seven to ten years' time?' Ben says everyone needs to ask themselves this question, no matter their relationship status.

A single, thirty-year-old rentvestor is going to be living a completely different life by the time they're forty. Maybe they get married and have a family, or perhaps they emerge, single, from a long-term relationship. Perhaps their salary increases dramatically, or they return to study, start a business or take an extended career break and move to Brazil. It's impossible to predict where life will take you, but the advantage of having an investment property is it gives you the freedom to grow, change and move as you please.

The challenge, Ben says, is what happens when it comes time to buy your second home, one that you'll perhaps want to live in. 'If you know you're going to want to buy a property in ten years, will you be able to save a 10 to 20 per cent deposit plus stamp duty?' That's on top of continuing to manage the costs of your first property.

In ten years' time you might need to sell, rather than keep the property and this can be a tough decision for people who've worked hard to purchase their first property. 'People can take three months to two years to sell,' Ben says. It often takes longer to sell if it didn't rise in value as the investor hoped, because it's emotionally taxing to part with a bad investment.

From first investment to family home

Vyvyan Hammond-Russell was renting in Sydney when the global financial crisis hit in 2007–08. While much of the media focus was on the impact this had on investors, little was said about the implications for renters. If investors had to sell, renters were inevitably given notice. 'I moved six times in two years. It was really expensive and very frustrating moving so often,' she says.

After yet another move, Vyv's mum had a knee replacement. Soon after, her other leg was injured in a car accident and she was left unable to walk. Vyv's mother needed her help. So Vyv moved out of a sharehouse and into her mum's one-bedroom apartment. Undoubtably a sacrifice, but she used the opportunity to save everything she earned working in social media for big brands.

'Nothing quite motivates you like sleeping on a fold-out couch in a 50-square-metre apartment with your mum,' Vyv, now thirty-five, says. But she adds, 'I managed to save $30,000.' Her family matched her savings, giving her $30,000 to add to her deposit. It wasn't something she'd expected, and she admits she was fortunate: 'That was a big deal; my family has never had any money.' It gave her a deposit of about 15 per cent and she used lender's mortgage insurance to make up the remaining 5 per cent. At that time, in 2011, she also had access to a $7000 first-homebuyer's grant and didn't have to pay stamp duty.

Despite that, it wasn't easy to buy. Looking in Surry Hills, one of the most expensive suburbs in the most expensive city in the country, was a nightmare. Vyv was determined to buy somewhere central. That meant buying small, but what her future home might lack in space it would more than make up for in proximity to the city, cafes and transport. Like me, she was ultimately looking for an investment, but it still had to be big enough to live a little – so she 'would always have somewhere to go back to.'

Securing that proved elusive. On one day she set herself the challenge of viewing nine properties. She found that one-bedroom units were going for anywhere between $400,000 and $500,000, depending on how new they were, while tiny studios were selling for between $350,000 and $400,000.

A run-down studio in a converted warehouse had her swooning. Yes, it was petite and needed work, but she was looking for a drawcard – something that made it stand out from the rest. Because it had originally been a warehouse, the ceilings were significantly higher, so although it was technically a studio the bedroom was separated by a mezzanine, making it feel like it had two rooms. It also had one of the few balconies in the building and much lower owners corporation fees than other apartments in the area. This meant her investment would stand out from the generic shoeboxes on offer in the area's new developments if she ever needed to sell. And with a purchase price of $360,000 it was 'unique in terms of cost'.

While she intended to live in it at first, Vyv thought beyond her-self and considered the lifestyles of future tenants. 'I assumed in the end the person who was renting it was going to be a single person or a young couple,' she recalls. 'Just because you're buying a home, doesn't mean it has to be your home forever.'

Not long after she moved into her studio, Vyv met Pete, the man who'd later become her husband. Pete, now thirty-seven, works in exhibitions and events as a project manager. He and his mate had bought a two-bedroom apartment for approximately $580,000 back in 2005. It was in Wollstonecraft, on Sydney's lower north shore, about 4 kilometres from the CBD – a crafty move. The friends moved into it straight after they finished university and never had to rent. While they paid off their mortgage, which was equivalent to rent anyway, prices skyrocketed.

Pete's friend got married a few years later and moved out, so a new flatmate moved in, covering his share. When the new flatmate announced his plans to move out in 2013, Pete asked Vyv if she'd like to live with him. 'He really put the pressure on,' she says, jokingly. But in truth, it was actually a difficult financial decision. She'd been planning to renovate the studio so it would be an attractive option on the rental market, but it wasn't quite ready. Using some savings and refinancing her loan to borrow an extra $10,000 in equity, Vyv com-mitted to getting the project done. She arranged a builder to replace the carpet with floorboards and install a fresh, white kitchen as well as some modern pendant lights in the living space. All up she spent about $33,000. With that sorted, she moved in with Pete and put her Surry Hills studio on the rental market.

Vyv and Pete married in 2015 and their housing plans began to shift. While the apartment was nice and quiet, it wasn't child-friendly. They knew bringing a baby into the world called for new living arrange-ments. 'It was pretty obvious to me that buying a proper house in

Sydney with a yard and enough space for kids was not going to be an easy feat,' Vyv says. Even with both of their investments as leverage, they'd been priced out of the city.

When the couple met, Pete worked just south of Wollongong and commuted up to two hours each way, every day; he later changed roles, to a position in Hurstville, 16 kilometres south of Sydney's CBD. Vyv believed he'd be open to moving further out and commuting again, as long as the drive wasn't worse than what he'd done in the past. But choosing a location to lay foundations more permanently wasn't easy. This was a long-term decision. Once they settled, that'd be their home for the foreseeable future.

'When I was young, I had a friend who lived at Coalcliff and I remembered going down to her place and thinking it was magical,' Vyv recalls, so she began to explore prices in the area. Coalcliff is a small coastal town on the Illawarra coast, about a 75-minute drive from Sydney. The area was undeniably beautiful. It had quiet beaches and long stretches of parkland – an idyllic place to raise children. 'It did, however, take me showing Pete a lot of houses to convince him to move out of the North Shore,' she adds.

By early 2016, after much research and exploration, Pete was on board. He sold the Wollstonecraft home, the profits from which Pete and his mate split down the line, and Vyv and Pete bought a three-bedroom home in Stanwell Park, not far from Coalcliff. Their property is 700 metres from the beach. Its rooms are filled with a bright light they'd never get in the city. And they paid $140,000 less than what Pete's apartment sold for. Weekday road trips are a small price to pay for long lazy weekends at the park or beach with their son, Odin.

Given they'd both used first-homebuyer concessions already, Pete and Vyv needed to come up with stamp duty as well as the deposit. To purchase the home, they used profits from Pete's sale as well as funds Vyv had saved working in a well-paying social media contract role with eBay. She'd decided not to dip into Surry Hills equity again. Good thing they made the leap. In January 2017, Stanwell Park had the highest regional growth nationally, with median prices rising 59.9 per cent from January 2016 to January 2017, to a hefty $1.57 million. The spike can be attributed in part to so many young people being priced out of Sydney, opting for regional locations instead and sucking up the commute.

Vyv continues to hold onto her Surry Hills studio and thinks about it as a very long-term investment – for when her small children eventually head to uni. 'I don't think anyone's kids will be able to afford to live in the city while they study. I'd like my kids to have this option, if they ever want to go to uni in Sydney. Hopefully I can make enough money to pay it off one day,' she says. Her advice for people considering rentvesting as a step into the market is, 'buy what you can afford, instead of what you can borrow. Once I bought, I realised how many extra costs there were upfront: legal fees, insurance and set-up fees can creep up on you.' In Vyv's case, the short-term pain was worth it for the long-term gain. She now has growing equity, and an emergency city base as well as the family home she dreamed of.

Avos of wisdom

 When you buy a small investment, your aim isn't necessarily to pay down a thirty-year loan. It's to maximise equity and use it as a stepping stone to your next property.

 Carefully research suburbs and make sure you're choosing a location that will generate a good rental yield. If you're considering purchasing interstate, it can pay to engage an expert who knows the market.

 Think about where you might be a decade from now. Vyv's experience shows that not everyone leverages their first investment to purchase a family home down the track.

 Consider ways you might save an additional deposit and stamp duty if you're not able to rely on the equity from your first investment straight away.

6

Changing the Property Game

FOR MANY PEOPLE, EVEN BUYING an investment property might seem like a lofty goal. So it's no surprise that young people are steering away from the traditional path to home ownership and investment. These clever folks are experimenting with new ways to get into the market – in many cases without giving up their values or lifestyles. This means reinventing the concept of rentvesting and purchasing unique or unexpected dwelling types, particularly for their value as short-term holiday rentals on accommodation platforms such as Airbnb. Want to live in a barn, on a boat, in a campervan or at a campsite? Crafty entrepreneurs are not only using the popularity of unconventional holiday experiences as a way to conquer the property market, they're becoming successful small business owners, too.

Renovating to rent

It's a cloudless spring day at 'The Barn', Heathcote, in central Victoria. Recent rain has cleared any pollution away and the timber structure looks commanding against the bright blue sky. I get out of the car, unclip the gate and rumble up the path. Jacob Stammers is out the back, preparing to convert a run-down shed into a bar ahead of his wedding to partner Brad, while his Jack Russell–Chihuahua, Harper, darts around next to him. In two weeks, forty guests will witness the couple tie the knot on their property, next to the dam they hope to some day turn into a natural swimming hole.

Heathcote is magnificent wine country not too far from the historic town of Bendigo. It's completely peaceful, aside from the occasional car driving down the nearby dirt road, and there's nothing but the sound of birds singing and a handful of flies buzzing around. Kangaroos casually bound around in the distance. Despite this rural vibe, it's an easy drive from Melbourne – I've done it in less than ninety minutes. After a hectic week in the city you'd be hard-pressed to find a better escape. Opening the heavy side door, we're treated to the subtle scent of a recent open fire. There's a rustic kitchen, big dining table, and a white timber staircase leading to a romantic mezzanine. An additional bed downstairs faces the large double barn doors, while packed bookcases and a large high-backed cane chair are calling out for a whole heap of lazing around.

It didn't look like this when Jacob and Brad laid eyes on it for the first time. Back in 2016, when they travelled from their East St Kilda rental to see the six-acre property with nothing but a barn on it, they weren't even seriously shopping. The pair wanted to explore alternatives to buying in the city, having already ruled out moving to the outer 'burbs. 'We were looking for a place with potential for rental income down the track within a couple of hours of Melbourne,' he explains. But then it happened ... He grins, 'We fell in love with the barn.'

It fitted the brief, except for the fact that it was little more than four walls and a roof on a massive patch of grass. 'It was very much a shell. It had the mezzanine in place, but it was untouched. It needed a lot of work to make it what it is today,' Jacob says. That's an understatement. Pictures of the original property reveal exposed insulation and a dirt floor. It was unfit for human habitation. And the asking price was $220,000. Despite that, Jacob, now thirty-five and Brad, twenty-nine, saw the potential. They had some funds, but even if they somehow managed to get hold of the place, more money would be needed for a barnyard blitz. But buying something liveable in their Melbourne hood was off the cards anyway. 'The house next to our rental in East St Kilda went up for auction and went for just under $900,000. It needed hundreds of thousand of dollars spent on it,' Jacob says. 'That was the moment of our realisation that we wouldn't be buying anywhere we wanted to live in a hurry.' So, it was barn or bust.

Getting a loan was always going to be a challenge. Jacob owns Mr Tucker, a cafe in North Melbourne. Self-employment was a first strike on his application, even though his income was steady and Brad had a stable role as a designer in the fashion industry.

They consulted Jacob's mum, who agreed to go guarantor. But they hit a roadblock four days out from settlement. Around that time, some banks were tightening their lending for suburbs identified as risky. Unsurprisingly, a block with an uninhabitable barn didn't fill the folks at the bank with calm confidence. An approved loan would be limited to 70 per cent of the property's value, meaning Jacob and Brad needed a 30 per cent deposit, even though their parents had offered to go guarantor. With the help of family they found the funds, but it came down to the wire. 'It was a stressful four days, but we managed to pull it off,' Jacob recalls. Victoria has generous incentives to buy regionally – a $20,000 first-homeowner's grant if you're buying something new. But this story is a reminder that not all regional properties are treated equally. Each lender has specific criteria. Jacob and Brad's experience is a reminder to do your research into what banks think about your chosen area before you commit to it.

But it turned out to be worth hustling for. In November 2016, they achieved their dream of owning a country property. Now all they had to do was make it financially viable. They'd done the sums and were in a position to pay their parents back their contribution within five years, while also managing the mortgage.

'We went into it with a view that if we never rented it, we were happy if it was a recreational thing for us. Being a country property, it's a pretty modest mortgage. It was manageable on our salaries,' he says. In fact, Jacob and Brad found it relatively easy to manage a small mortgage and continue to rent where they wanted to live. It made them reassess their spending habits. 'It just shows how much money you do waste.'

With that insight processed, they got their hands dirty. 'It had water pumps, electricity and NBN, funnily enough,' but that was about it. After overseeing the design of a couple of cafe interiors, Jacob had developed a strong eye, and Brad of course made a living surrounded by stylish design. A further plus: Jacob has a builder brother who was generous with his advice. 'My brother had the tools and was available for phone support. He came out for a couple of days. It made it possible to do it ourselves.'

It wasn't easy though. Painting the place white took four days and a hard-working spray gun. 'I had to go to Bendigo three times to get more paint. It was thirsty wood,' Jacob remembers.

They spent a bit under $50,000 on the renovation. So, for a total of $270,000 they had a refitted barn that sleeps four on a beautiful property and it was ripe for rental. All that spending meant that a listing on Airbnb was a necessity – they hoped to recover at least some of their costs.

The annual Heathcote show, which attracts visitors each November, was coming up. It'd been twelve months since they'd bought, and they were ready to test their unconventional investment on the general public. At $200 per night, it wasn't a cheap offering.

But it was beautiful, and the bookings flowed in. 'It ticked along for the next few months after that,' Jacob says.

What do their parents think about their investment? 'My mum is blown away,' Jacob says. Back when she viewed the property prior to settlement she was 'overwhelmed' by the job they faced, but she backed her entrepreneurial son and his partner. 'You had a vision. You saw the potential in it,' Jacob remembers her saying. Soon, they became Airbnb superhosts, meaning they were among the most trusted listings on the site.

This is just the beginning. Brad and Jacob have plans to put a container studio at the back of the property near the budding orchard. In another spot, they want to build a two-bedroom A-frame home. Then there's their plan for a cedar sauna, landscaped garden and outdoor entertaining area. It'll be a rustic resort in no time.

If you're thinking about following in their regional footsteps, Jacob says 'proceed with caution'. Turning their investment into a profitable venture took time. You need to be sure you can fund the mortgage repayments before it starts generating cashflow. Plus, it's harder to get a loan for a regional block. 'The banks have a different metric based on how long the properties sit on the market for,' Jacob explains.

Using short-term stays to build equity faster

For better or worse, short-term accommodation is part of the property-market tapestry, and people are using it to assist the transition to ownership. You can take a slow-burn approach like Jacob and Brad, or you can build equity fast like Rebecca Warden and Dan Khouzam.

It started with a bluestone cottage in the Adelaide suburb of Stepney. In 2014, when they laid eyes on this beauty, other prospective buyers were giving it a glance and strolling on by. The area was semi-industrial and that wasn't attractive to those seeking traditional residential streetscapes. 'We were like "nah, this is an awesome area" and the price for us was really good,' Bec says.

The bluestone facade and its extremely reasonable $410,000 price tag made it the perfect first home for Bec, then twenty-four, and Dan, who was twenty-six. 'We saved by working some seriously long hours and just made sure to be very careful with our spending,' she explains. The two-bedroom, one-bathroom property had a sweet courtyard and only needed surface cosmetic work, like a fresh coat of paint and new carpet. Some plumbing fixes were required, so for a while it was a bit like camping. 'If we had to go to the bathroom, we'd come to the office,' she laughs.

Pretty soon, South Australians caught on to semi-industrial style and demand began to push prices up. Within two years, Bec and Dan had enough equity and savings to purchase a second property in Norwood, a desirable eastern suburb. This place was renovated and didn't need much additional work, so they moved in, renting the Stepney bluestone to trustworthy mates. But once ensconced in Norwood, they realised they could potentially make some extra cash listing their new house for occasional holiday rental. 'We chucked it on Airbnb for a laugh,' Bec recalls.

'People don't realise there are people coming to their city every week.' Bec and Dan had been in Norwood for about three months and demand for good Airbnb rentals was on the up. At first they just took the occasional booking, throwing their belongings into the car and staying at Bec's folks' place. But soon their gear was being shoved in car boots so frequently they decided to make Norwood a full-time Airbnb listing. 'Everyone thought we were crazy, but we knew how much demand there was,' Bec says.

They're a financially savvy pair. Dan runs a business called Signature Wines, which Bec worked in until recently. She now has her own social media and marketing business. On top of both of their incomes, the Norwood Airbnb brings in far more than it would as a traditional rental. If they'd chosen permanent tenants through the rental market, they'd be receiving about $500 per week. On Airbnb, they can achieve $240 per night. Um, yeah. Let me do the maths for you. *That's $1640 per week* (less Airbnb's listing fees). Not only did this bring in the coin needed to pay their mortgage and tax on the income, there was enough left over to save.

Sleeping at her parents' house was never going to be a permanent arrangement though, so later that year Bec and Dan bought a one-bedroom unit in nearby St Peters, where they could live while they plotted their next move. Thanks to their incomes and the excess Airbnb funds, they had enough to buy. This tiny 42-square-metre place was a temporary space of their own until they bought their next project, in turn making the unit another Airbnb.

For the St Peter's unit they'd get somewhere between $200 and $300 per week in rent. Currently, it brings in nearly $1000 per week on Airbnb.

Meanwhile, they tackled a massive renovation at a new site in Unley, which they nabbed in 2017.

Despite running their own businesses and planning a wedding, they did all the demolition work, painting and insulating themselves. 'Our advice would be to do as much as you can yourself. We spent about a year living in basically two rooms, with no kitchen or cleaning facilities at all – it is amazing how much you can adapt when you really have to,' Bec suggests. Surely with all that income from the other properties they could have outsourced the work? No, Bec says, 'we got quotes from builders and there was no way'. They've done some of the expensive work themselves and arranged tradies in stages, so they weren't hit with a huge bill in one shot.

Putting hard-earned properties on Airbnb isn't foolproof, though. At 10.30 pm one night in October 2018, Bec got a call from the cops.

They politely informed her that the Norwood Airbnb was currently occupied by an opportunistic high school student who was charging entry to her home. An open event on Facebook had attracted hundreds of teenagers.

The couple arrived to assess the carnage. 'It had been trashed. Every room. There were hundreds of empty Cruiser bottles and they'd put furniture in the garden,' Bec says. It got worse, too. 'We couldn't kick them out straight away because some kids were so sick they had to go to hospital.' Eventually, when the students had been ejected and the cops left, Bec and Dan started cleaning. They scrubbed until 3 am, then got up early and restored the home to its immaculate pre-party state, finishing by midday – just in time for the next guest to arrive.

Normally they have a cleaner who looks after their properties, but in this instance there wasn't time, and the demands of the party-scale clean-up made it unreasonable to ask someone else to do the dirty work. Despite that experience, Bec's not fazed about keeping it as an Airbnb. But they are now more discerning when selecting guests.

They're considering putting Unley on Airbnb, now that they've finished renovating there, too. But first, they'll kick back and reap the rewards of their hard work. Quite rightly, I say. 'We want to be a bit smart at this stage; we've done what we can afford,' Bec concludes.

What to consider for short-term rentals

These stories might make it sound like using Airbnb, Riparide and other short-stay sites is an easy way to make money, but setting up a holiday rental takes careful planning and a cash injection at the beginning. Before you go leaping into it, there's stuff you need to know.

Generally, you can charge more for a short-term rental than you can for a permanent rental, which means you'll get better returns. But that only works if you're taking bookings regularly. So the key is to choose a location where there's demand all the time. Think handy inner-city locations close to prized amenities, as well as picturesque regional spots that have year-round tourism demand. To get an idea of an area's potential, jump on Airbnb and look at the listings: check the number of properties, monitor their occupancy rates, and see what properties similar to yours are going for to make sure you're setting a competitive price. You may want to set your price slightly lower than established hosts until you have reviews and a good star rating.

You'll also want to look at the pros and cons of deriving income from avenues such as Airbnb. The extra money that you make from your rental will be taxable if it is positively geared (that is, generating more income than the investment costs you). However, there are tax deductions on things such as utilities, interest on your mortgage, property management and repairs to offset that. Before you commit, talk to a tax specialist to understand what's at stake, what you can deduct and how much you might owe when it comes time to lodge your tax return.

It's important to research the Airbnb guidelines in your state, too. As governments look to impose regulations to protect communities, some new restrictions are falling into place. In Sydney, for example, new planning laws limit the number of days investors can rent their homes as short-term rentals to 180 days per year. Regional locations in New South Wales, however, are not impacted by the change. In Tassie, property owners need permits for holiday homes, investment properties and dwellings with more than four bookable rooms,

Set-up costs

Unlike a private rental, your property must come fully furnished, so you'll need to budget for everything from bedding to kitchen utensils. Think of the things you expect from a rental: washing facilities, TV, wifi. Setting up a whole home – especially one that looks good enough to compete with other attractive homes – isn't cheap, so be prepared for some significant early outlay.

Having said that, you can get creative on that front. If your property has more of a rustic aesthetic, you could get away with furniture from markets, garage sales or the side of the road; grab second-hand items on buy, swap and sell sites; scour bargain auction houses and op-shops.

Marketing

You need to create a listing that stands out, so professional-looking photos are essential. Either take the pics yourself with a high-quality camera or use Airbnb's service. Simply apply for a photographer and they'll send someone to get the snaps that work best on the site. Rather than paying for these, Airbnb deducts the cost from the income you make on your first few bookings. Just ensure the pictures are a true representation of what people can expect to find when they arrive. If the images don't match reality, you're on a fast-track to poor reviews and you risk losing out on future bookings.

Property management costs

Short-term stays have become so lucrative that new property management businesses have popped up to provide services for time-poor homeowners. They can do everything from communicating with prospective guests to check-ins and cleaning. But outsourcing this will eat into your profits, so shop around and see if you can strike a good deal. Some companies will take 15 per cent for basic services; others charge 20 per cent or more.

You can opt to do the property management yourself, but while you save funds in avoiding outsourcing, you lose time. If you have a demanding job, it's going to be tough to reply to all the requests and queries in a timely fashion, clean your property immaculately, wash and replace linen after each visit and check in the next guests, especially if this is happening during office hours. Realistically, it's probably best to get some assistance – unless some other factors make this convenient for you (perhaps you work part-time or have taken some kind of long work hiatus). You're essentially running a hospitality business, so you need to think about whether you're suited to this. Do you have time to plump the pillows, keep the plants alive, trim the hedges, and manage the admin and insurance?

It's a good idea to have a bit of cash in your back pocket for unexpected maintenance. If you want quality guests to leave great reviews, your place has to be delightful at all times – and so, in your dealings with guests, do you.

Reducing private rental stock

It's great if you can make more money out of your investment via Airbnb than through the traditional private rental system, but consider this: spikes in Airbnb-style short-stay accommodation can reduce the amount of private rentals available. You mightn't care. You're not a charity after all. But a rising short-term housing trend in some parts of the country – particularly in places where demand for holiday accommodation is high – will inevitably reduce options for renters seeking long-term homes.

In March 2018, during an emerging housing summit in Hobart, the Tasmanian government announced that more than 200 hectares of Crown land would be released for residential development as a way to combat dangerously low rental vacancies. The rental shortage mixed with rising house prices had resulted in some families pitching tents in the Hobart Showgrounds. The Hobart example is telling. Tassie now attracts Australian and international tourists, with many coming to see MONA, tour wineries and trek through magnificent national parks. Landlords are cottoning on, listing homes on Airbnb in huge numbers. There are more than 300 options in Hobart alone, with some commanding more than $250 per night, while the average three-bedroom home might bring in $450 per week as a long-term rental. It's easy to see why landlords are cashing in on Airbnb.

Tassie's private rental market became so bad that in April 2018, housing minister Roger Jaensch proposed to offer landlords between $10,000 and $13,000 to rent their homes privately and guaranteed to have the rent paid for the term of the lease in order to increase rental stock, particularly for low-income earners. A pilot program was launched and the aim was to have 110 properties available by June 2019.

Avos of wisdom

 Brad and Jacob were lucky to secure an unconventional regional property. If you're looking at regional options, talk to your bank or mortgage broker about the associated loan requirements. You don't want to fall in love with a remote shack only to find the bank deems it too risky to proceed with.

 Short-term rentals can be listed at a higher price than long-term private rentals, but you'll only get a better return if they're booked solidly, and they involve a lot of work. Choose your location wisely and be prepared for upfront costs and major time expenditure.

7

Research for Motivation and Success

SAVING IS BORING AND IT takes bloody ages. Many of us who've been raised on a diet of instant gratification struggle with working towards such long-term goals. But I assure you that one minute you're looking at a bank balance comprised of a few cents and then, out of nowhere, you've ticked over to five figures. I remember the day I transferred another $1500 into my savings account and the amount hit $10,000. *Holy shit, I'm doing it*, I thought. And if I can do it, you can too.

For the first month or two, I was powered by the shame of having wasted so much money – that and gratitude for the opportunity to return home. This inspired a short, initial burst of 'guilt-saving'. By the third month, though, sitting on the couch watching *The Living Room* on a Friday night, asking permission to have another glass of wine to get through it, I was contemplating pulling the pin. It wasn't worth it. My friends were out enjoying themselves, living their best years without me, while I was scrolling through Instagram and Facebook, living

91

vicariously on the sad side of a smartphone screen. At least, I told myself, I wouldn't be hungover on Saturday.

I'm no psychologist, but I don't think it takes one to tell you that the biggest barrier to saving is what's going on inside your noggin. Freaking out that I was now excluded from some epic, unmissable life moments wasn't doing me any favours. Whether you're living with your parents or in your own home, forgoing nights out in order to save requires a particular mental strength, especially in this age of social media–induced fomo.

I had to find things to do that would help me work towards my long-term goal and didn't cost me anything. And you know what? Aside from the cost of transportation, inspecting properties is free, baby!

This little lightbulb moment helped me realise I needed to do something constructive while I was saving: research. At this point, I still had no idea what I was working towards, which made it difficult to maintain motivation. A 2017 Westpac study showed that 65 per cent of millennials said they would save more if they had a specific goal in mind. This makes sense. Saving for 'a property' was too generic. I needed to know more clearly what my future investment might look like.

I knew I'd probably be buying an apartment and I understood that I would most likely have to move further out than I was accustomed to. But in which direction? I scrolled through listings on real estate websites and started to compare prices in various suburbs. I fell in love with tiny Art Deco apartments in Melbourne's inner east. One had a small bedroom and windows overlooking a leafy courtyard. But it had a communal laundry and a bathroom that needed work. It was also going to take more than twelve months of saving to secure it. In the west, I could get a two-bedroom apartment in a rundown block that I might be able to afford, but I didn't love the area.

An ad for a development in the inner-city suburb of Richmond caught my eye. I'd already been cautioned about buying off the plan, but the idea of a home that was brand spanking new was tempting. Maybe I could sacrifice space to actually buy where I wanted to live.

I got in the car the next morning to visit the display suite. The space, set up like one of the apartments, was definitely appealing. I ran my finger across a stone benchtop and imagined myself cooking here while my friends milled around, drinking wine. It was a picture-perfect image of what my life could look life. A grown-up doll's house. It was also an alluring trap.

One-bedroom apartment prices started at $380,000. Then there were the extremely high owners corporation fees thanks to the lift, pool and other amenities. My friends would have to sit on the couch for dinner. I doubted there was room for a dining table. It was an over-priced box wrapped in layer after layer of slick marketing.

'We'll take a 10 per cent deposit now and you can pay the rest on completion!' the agent informed me with excruciatingly fake enthusiasm. He handed me a glossy brochure. I wished he would stop grinning; it was really awkward. 'Thanks,' I replied, eyeballing him and refusing to return his smile. It was hard enough to wrap my head around the options – I didn't need the distracting smarmy performance.

I wondered how many people like me would be tempted by this deal, only to find later that the house they'd been sold didn't look anything like the pictures or the display suite – because the stone benchtop was a premium extra and the entry-level-priced units didn't have bedroom windows. As I walked out, I decided that a new apartment in a suburb I actually wanted to live in was definitely off the agenda. I needed to buy smart. The key to purchasing in a market where prices were already astronomical had to be stepping backwards to move forward. I resolved to find a place that mightn't be my first preference but that would grow in value over time. If I was going to put myself through hell, it had better be bloody worth it.

Understanding the market

Zoe and Matt Bonwick had five years of research under their belts before they bought their home. Although they didn't secure a property until April 2016, Zoe, a graphic designer, had been checking listings every single week since 2011. That's a serious commitment. Fortunately, those long years of research would come in handy when it really mattered.

The newlyweds married in 2015 and continued living in a sharehouse in the Melbourne suburb of Richmond after they got hitched. They didn't mind living with other people if it meant being able to save more for a family home. Plus, they loved the location and making a household with their mates. There was no rush to shack up alone.

But a getaway to the country races just when they were ready to start bidding for properties put a spanner in the works. Late at night, just ten minutes from their destination, 'a kangaroo came bounding up and straight into the headlights,' Zoe remembers. They got the car fixed, but it was old, and after the accident it kept overheating. The damage was done. They sold the car to a Volkswagen repair guy.

A new car wasn't in the financial plan – not ideal when they were spending their Saturdays trying to pack as many inspections and auctions into the day as possible. So, what are a couple of househunting lovebirds on a budget to do? Get on their bikes, that's what. Their Saturdays were now carefully plotted according to how far they could feasibly travel with pedal power. 'We'd ride 40 to 50 kilometres,' Zoe says. Luckily, they were both thirty-two – young enough to get away with rolling up to auction battles in lycra.

'We would have looked so funny. We were bidding hundreds of thousands and then when we missed out, we'd ride off on our bikes,' she says. But it wasn't funny. By the time they started bidding, they'd narrowed down their search exclusively to Northcote, in Melbourne's inner north. At that time, the median house price there was more than

$950,000 and competition was intense. Zoe and Matt had saved their deposit without family help, but they often lost out to other young couples who had their parents standing behind them. After one particularly heartbreaking auction, at which they were once again outbid, they rode home miserable. 'I was teary, Matt was cranky,' Zoe recalls.

Still, the expertise accumulated. Every week without a successful bid was another chance to clock up a bit more understanding about what the market was doing. They'd assess floor plans, compare results and study the properties that were passed in.

'When you sell a car, it has to be roadworthy – if you want a building inspection, you have to pay for that. You can't get a building inspection on fifty houses,' she points out. At more than $300 a pop, they're definitely costly, so understanding what a building inspector looks for can be invaluable. However, it's possible to negotiate a building inspection before signing on the dotted line, so you're not forking out for an inspection until you're close to buying a property. When you make a preliminary offer on a property, you can state certain conditions. The two most common conditions are 'subject to finance', meaning you still need final loan approval, and 'subject to a pest or building inspection', which gives you time to arrange a proper going-over of the property before the offer is officially agreed to by both parties.

Zoe and Matt started quizzing building inspectors about the key issues to look out for. Over time, their own inspections became as detailed as possible. To others who are deep in the research phase, Zoe suggests understanding what professional building inspectors look for: everything from dodgy taps to signs of mould.

Eventually, it was their turn. On a Sunday in May 2016, their legs sore from the previous day of riding and their hopes dashed once again, Matt read the auction results and found a couple of properties that had been passed in – including one they hadn't even looked at, because 'you can't get to everything', Zoe says. The next morning, Monday, Zoe got up and rode to work in the rain. Matt insisted she had to make the 5 pm inspection he'd arranged, even if it meant working through lunch to leave early and riding to the property in the damp clothes that had been sitting in her bag all day. It turned out to be worth it.

She arrived at the little Victorian terrace that needed some work and they wandered through. It was already getting dark. An inspection that occurs outside daylight hours is certainly not advisable, because you can't see cracks in the walls or mould, but their comprehensive research enabled Zoe and Matt to make an informed decision. 'We knew one around the corner had gone for a similar price, and this one had an extra bedroom and a carpark, too,' she says. They made an offer that night.

By Wednesday, it was theirs. The fact that it had been passed in meant they got a competitive price and could reserve a small amount of funds to do a bit of the necessary work to the place. Soon the young couple would finally move out of their sharehouse and into their own home. Today, they've also managed to get a car and become a family of three. They're glad they had to stick at the search for so long; it gave them the confidence to negotiate on a home that was both a good investment and a place they'll live happily for years to come. Their son, Harvey, came through the door for the first time in October 2018.

Do you need a mortgage broker?

The role of a good mortgage broker is to go to a number of banks and look at suitable loan options for your requirements. They'll assess your financial capacity to see what can be achieved, and they'll have a comprehensive understanding of the bank's current requirements for a loan.

There are plenty of advantages to engaging this type of specialist. Mortgage brokers will explore more loan options than your current bank might provide, and uncover opportunities that you mightn't have been aware of. They're equipped with the understanding and resources to do all the mortgage research on your behalf and structure the best possible loan for your specific needs. They can save you a lot of time because they're across all the options, and they should make sure you get a competitive interest rate. They also know exactly what the bank will look for when it comes time to assess your application, and they'll help you to prepare the necessary documentation.

However, mortgage brokers are paid a commission by banks and credit unions. In the past, some might have only recommended the financial institutions that would enable them to get their cut, which is why it's important to shop around before you select a broker. Somewhat notoriously, mortgage brokers have been known to secure larger loans than their customers could really afford in some cases. Fortunately, since the 2018 royal commission into banking and the financial services industry, this practice has come under sharper scrutiny. As part of your loan application, banks will now do a comprehensive stress test on your ability to save and manage a loan.

Whether you use a mortgage broker or not, it's still essential to do your own research and ensure any recommendations you get line up with what you can actually afford. Ultimately, Dad and I had a clear understanding of what I needed, so we didn't work with a broker. Instead, we chose a bank that we had an existing relationship with, and I understood the staff there would assess my income, spending, savings, credit card debt and my overall financial capacity for borrowing.

When to bid

People shopping for new digs in the desirable suburbs of Surry Hills, Redfern and Waterloo, Sydney, are caught in the eye of the auction storm. Here, a tiny one-bedroom with timber floors and bright white walls can go for more than $800,000. Buyers are lucky if they get a balcony or a courtyard. If you want a three-bedroom Victorian terrace, you're looking at $2,000,000, easily.

In spite of that, some first home buyers are still eager to bid. According to agent Mark Foy, the key to knowing whether to bid is to understand what's happening in the market at the time you're planning to buy. He's Sydney-based, but these rules apply everywhere. 'The one question millennials should ask is: are we in a bull market or a bear market?'

In a bull market, prices are going up and the demand for properties is high, so auctions produce good results for vendors and agents alike. In a bull market, it's a good idea to try to secure the house before it goes to auction. But if agents know there are a couple of really keen parties, they might decline a very decent pre-auction offer knowing that competition will push the selling price up on the day.

In a bear market, prices are falling, and vendors may choose to sell before the market declines any further. 'In this case you're better off waiting and going to the auction. You could be one of two buyers anyway,' Mark says. A crowded auction doesn't always equal a rowdy bidding-fest, especially in a cooling market. 'Unless it's a cracker of a property. Even in a bear market, you're going to see some competition for quality homes.'

This might sound obvious, but when you go to an auction, you need to be the last bidder if you want to win. If the property gets passed in, he explains, it puts you in the best position to negotiate. 'The more buyers that bid, the higher the prices go.' When this happens, he says, 'sit back' until bidding has almost come to a close. That's when you can bid – if it's still within your budget, that is.

If the property is passed in and you're the highest bidder, we give you the opportunity to negotiate,' Foy says. If the vendor doesn't take your offer, then negotiations with other interested parties occur.

Making an offer before auction

Want a better price? Just make an offer beforehand, right?

Hang on, bucko. It's not that simple. Mark says that if there's interest, the auction will probably go ahead unless your offer blows them out of the water – like, it's not just at the top end of the advertised price range, it's well above it. When a vendor accepts an offer prior to auction, it's most likely because 'they only have one buyer and they're wrapping up a deal prior'.

Negotiating on a property that's been passed in

Is there something wrong with a property if it's been passed in?

Not necessarily, Mark says. He points out that properties can get passed in for a number of reasons: 'it's not presented well, there's heaps of other stock or they've skimped on marketing'. In some cases, it could be because the vendor's expectations of the sale value are too high. 'Agents sometimes tell vendors what they want to hear. People don't want to hear their property is worth less than it was a year ago,' he says. But, on the flipside, 'It could also mean the property has been unlucky.' There's every chance there's nothing wrong with it, but for whatever reason it's been overlooked by other buyers. That's when you pounce.

Making sure the price is right

Whether you make an offer before auction, bid on the day, negotiate after a property has been passed in, or try to secure a private sale, you really only have one job: understand the market. Be very clear on the kind of price that comparable properties are going for. Avoid getting overly emotional because you think you've found 'the one'. This is not a love story, it's an investment.

This is the time when it can really pay to engage a buyer's agent or someone who's able to negotiate on your behalf. They don't care how amazing your armchair is going to look in that sunny nook, they care about getting the best price, full stop. It may cost you a bit: they may charge a fee for the search and acquisition process, which could be 2 per cent of the purchase price, as well as negotiation and bidding fees. But if they save you tens of thousands because they were pragmatic and ruthless, their fees might pay for themselves.

Is off the plan off the agenda?

Look, I'm not going to tell you what sort of investment to buy. Properties of all shapes and sizes can make money over time. I know people who've bought off the plan, and over the two-year period that it takes to build their property, it's become worth more than it was when they paid their deposit.

However, there are some obvious risks. For one, you're making the biggest purchase of your life based on something you've seen in a brochure. You don't see the fixtures or fittings until you move in. Even if you think you've got a clear picture because you've seen the display suite, you can't tell exactly how light it will be or how small the bedroom will feel. You might not realise how paper-thin the walls are until you're living next door to a dude who plays techno at all hours.

The appeal of off-the-plan apartments lies in the fact that they're brand-new and often in desirable suburbs. Maybe there's a pool and a rooftop garden and a sleek lift to your apartment that has city views! Yeah, cool, but you will pay a fortune for these features in owners corporation fees. Have you budgeted for that?

'I'm a first home buyer and I get massive concessions for buying something brand-new,' you tell me. I hear you. I had the same thought. But what's the point in saving $10,000 on your purchase if you pay too much for a property in an area that has an oversupply of apartments half a decade later? Oversupply is the last thing you want. If it's an investment, it means you could struggle to find a tenant or have to reduce the rent due to lack of demand. If you're an owner-occupier and find yourself in a position where you need to sell, you run the risk of reduced demand due to the healthy level of supply.

Oh, and those city views they sold you in the brochure? By the time your apartment's ready, there's a new development across the road, so your view is actually a concrete wall. Tough break.

Read the fine print

It could be tempting to drop a 10 per cent deposit and buy off the plan, knowing that you don't need to pay the balance until settlement, which could be years away. That gives you time to save the rest, and stock up on reserve money to manage the mortgage when you eventually move in. But once you sign that contract, you're locked in. So, if you're considering it, engage a conveyancer or solicitor to review the document first. The biggest leap of faith you can take is signing a contract years before you apply for the loan. If for any reason you can't proceed to settlement, the developer can potentially take your deposit and charge a shortfall. For example, if you agreed to purchase a $400,000 apartment and you paid a $40,000 deposit, but you default and they only make $350,000 on your property when they sell it to someone else, you could potentially owe another $10,000.

If off the plan is your way into the market, do your research. Not all made-to-order investments are the same. Research the developer's previous projects to see how they've performed. Look into plans for nearby developments that might be in the pipeline, which may impact the future level of supply. If you're purchasing as an investor, you don't want to arrive at settlement only to find there are more apartments than people willing to rent them.

Refine your wish list

During my research phase I spoke to heaps of people who'd bought all sorts of homes. I asked them what they'd learned, what the challenges were and why they'd chosen that particular suburb or type of house.

My mate Simon, who works in property, told me the key was to look in suburbs that are 'flying under the radar'. Richmond's prices had exploded years earlier, so it wasn't the smartest suburb to buy in if I wanted to see growth fast. He pointed to Melbourne's outer bay-side suburbs, such as Parkdale, Mordialloc and Bonbeach. There I'd find freestanding one-bedroom units for about $300,000, and larger two-bedroom apartments for less than $350,000. He told me that two bedrooms would increase the range of possible renters when it came time to list.

While this was a little further out of town than I would've liked to live, these suburbs came with pristine beaches, good schools attractive streetscapes and easy access to the Frankston train line, which could deliver workers to inner-city jobs. There, I'd get more bang for my investment buck and property values would hopefully rise as inner-city prices pushed more people out of town. The key, Simon explained, was to buy in a suburb before people realised it was a good deal.

So, having decided where to buy, I settled on the following non-negotiables.

A two-bedder

For starters, the bank might be hesitant to lend on a unit that's less than 50 or 60 square metres because resale on something so small can be a challenge. Having two bedrooms has multiple advantages. First, if you're living alone you can potentially rent the second room out, reducing the cost of your mortgage. And when it does come time to rent it out as an investment, you'll have a broader share of the market. One bedroom is only suitable for a single person or a couple. Two bedrooms allows for a family or friends looking to share a place.

That's not to say you should rule out one-bedrooms. If it suits your lifestyle and it's a great space in a good suburb, it can still be an excellent option. You need to weigh up your budget and long-term plans for the property.

Liveable, but not necessarily brand-new

My aim was to buy something that didn't need a thing done to it – but it didn't have to be perfect. Admittedly, it took me a while to get over this. I'd started Pinterest boards featuring kitchens with hexagon-tile splashbacks and designer pendant lights hanging over stone benchtops. I got obsessed with bathtubs and copper tap fittings. But those in the know told me repeatedly: you pay a premium for brand-new. I could add those features in time. For now, I needed functional, not fashionable.

In a suburb that was 'on the up'

I settled on Melbourne's outer bayside area. If I had to move more than 20 kilometres away from family and friends to get something affordable, it would at least be nice to have some lifestyle features like cafes and parks. Not to mention a couple of pubs and bars so I could lure friends for visits. Suburbs crammed with development and cranes were off the list. That wasn't to say my chosen suburbs were exempt from future development, but the key was to get in *before* the location became the next go-to for developers, first home buyers and savvy investors.

Pretty streetscapes

I knew I wouldn't be able to afford the best house in a given street, but as long as there were handsome homes, established trees and manicured nature strips nearby, I'd know that I was buying in an area where people were houseproud, and community was strong. This would naturally attract future buyers if and when I needed to sell. Although I was leaning towards an apartment, I still hoped I would find something in a quiet residential street, not a spot that was teeming with shopping centres and one big development after another.

Shops, schools, cafes and parks

Good-looking streets are a start, but quality schools, cafes and parks were also essential. Again, I had to think beyond myself to what a future renter or owner might need. Schools are a particularly powerful drawcard. People have kids.

Access to trains

Although I had a car, I knew that proximity to a trainline was essential. If you're a Melburnian, you'll be no stranger to the peak-hour squeeze, where people will pour themselves into carriages and hold their breath, exchanging body heat with strangers until they're ejected at their chosen station. A good trainline with express services that reduces the likelihood of being trapped in this scenario was another bonus.

And just like that, I had a clear motivation to save. It was enough to propel me forward, ignore the frustrations that came with living at my folks' house and turn down boozy nights with less anxiety and fomo. Not only did I know what I was working towards, I knew how I wanted to buy: in a private sale or after auction.

When it came time to actually buy in my selected area, it wasn't a full-blown bull market but there was definitely plenty of activity. I knew I needed to develop nerves of steel. I wasn't in a position to bid over my budget. If anything, I wanted to be able to negotiate a competitive price, so I'd probably avoid bidding wars completely.

Avos of wisdom

 It's hard to save when you don't know what you're saving for. Doing your research helps you get confident in your decision and creates a clear goal to work towards. You'll also become an expert in prices and make a better, more competitive offer when the time comes. Keep your eyes on the prize.

 Go to auctions and open for inspections well before you're ready to buy, that way you'll be clear on auction processes and you'll be better placed to make a smart offer.

 If you're considering buying off the plan, research the developer's history and look into other developments planned for the area. Avoid buying in an area at risk of oversupply.

 Learn as much as you can independently, but know when to engage specialists like mortgage brokers, building inspectors and buyers agents.

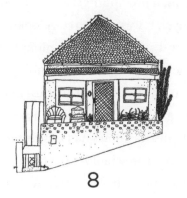

8

Paperwork, Paperwork, Paperwork

IT WAS A HOT DAY in January 2014, thirteen months after I'd moved home, when I started scrolling through property listings with more than just wistful hope. I was actually getting to a point where I had enough saved in the bank to apply for a mortgage. One place in Mordialloc, in Melbourne's south-east – the suburb I'd already set my sights on – earned a click.

The building itself, a two-storey block with six units, looked pretty basic. An older red brick structure with a tin roof, it needed some love. But a block of six was far more appealing than a block of thirty. As I worked my way through the pictures, I was struck by how clean and light the interior looked. It had two bedrooms and was surrounded by trees. I plugged the address into Google Maps and saw a quiet residential street, good schools and a golf course nearby. It was a short drive from the beach and not far from the train station. It was open for inspection that afternoon.

I continued my search, adding a few other addresses to make the drive to Mordialloc worthwhile, and reached for my car keys. At that point, I didn't have loan pre-approval and I still wasn't convinced I'd ever be a winning buyer. It was time to start looking beyond what I was seeing on property websites, though, to glimpse these places in real life. I envisioned rocking up to find a crumbling mess – not the polished pictures presented in the digital world – but still, I'd start to get a better sense of the gap between marketing and reality.

The street was wide. Its homes had freshly mown lawns and white picket fences. The two-storey building, set back behind a hedge, was the only block of apartments in the street. A cheery woman in a skirt suit holding a clipboard and some brochures stood at the door. 'Hello, sweetie,' she said, and asked for my name and phone number. Sweetie? *Lady, I'm not a six-year-old*, I wanted to say. I refrained, though, gave her my details and took a brochure.

As I stepped inside, I was stunned. It looked just like the pictures. It truly was large and light. I wandered into the bedroom, which was filled with the current tenant's junk, but I got the idea: my bed, bedside tables and armchair would fit nicely in the space. I imagined a spare bed in the second room and my desk under the window.

But why was I the only person looking? 'Oh, sweetie, everyone's at the beach!' She exclaimed. I hadn't thought about that. This was a good time to be inspecting. Who wants to drive around contemplating stuffy apartments when they could be dipping in and out of the bay between naps on the sand? A private sale in January might just result in a better price.

The owner needed to sell. It had been on the market more than once and he hadn't achieved his target. Now he just wanted to get rid of it. This was excellent news. I feigned indifference, though. Poker face was key. 'It's nice,' I said. 'I have a few other places I'm looking at ... I'll let you know.' I wandered down the stairs to the driveway.

Back in the car, I was quietly stoked. I turned up my tunes, pumped the air-con and smiled. If I could bargain them down, this would sit at the bottom end of my budget … But it was too soon to be thinking like that though. Who buys the first place they look at? Surely I was getting ahead of myself.

Motoring further down the Nepean Highway to Aspendale, I pulled up at my next inspection. A small two-bedroom unit. I felt like I'd entered a retirement village. It turns out I had. Well, not exactly, but the agent looked confused when I gave him my details. 'You have to be over fifty-five to buy this place – you realise that, don't you?'

Um, what?

I hadn't read the fine print in the listing. This property was zoned for retirement, which meant only older folks could make an offer. I didn't even know that was a thing. So here the boomers are with all the property already, but there are still some areas reserved exclusively for them? How was that fair? I mean, I liked Phil Collins as much as the next person; it seemed outrageously ageist.

'Where are the ones for poor young people under thirty-five?' I joked.

'You're welcome to look around while you're here,' he replied, unmoved. I had a quick squiz and got the hell out of there. I drove home via Beach Road and thought more about the Mordialloc place. I probably shouldn't rule it out purely because it was the first one I'd seen. I could imagine re-commencing my adult life there.

Back at home, I showed Dad the place and he agreed it seemed to be a good buy. We created a spreadsheet so I could see what my options were, depending on what I was able to negotiate. The numbers were terrifying. Deposit, stamp duty, lender's mortgage insurance (because I didn't have a 20 per cent deposit) and conveyancing. That was all before I started footing the regular bill for the mortgage, covered moving costs, owners corporation fees and more. 'If you can get it for less than $320,000, you're in a good position,' Dad insisted.

Led by faith in the almighty spreadsheet, we returned a week later to inspect the property together. This time, my new agent buddy talked directly to Dad. I felt stupid, but truthfully I had no idea what I was doing. I needed the help and I was grateful to have it. This time, we took a copy of the section 32 and it was time to get my head around that.

The vendor statement

The vendor statement, also known as the section 32, is a document that covers everything you need to know about your prospective investment, including the particulars of the title, council and body corporate rates, water, and any covenants on the property (legal restrictions outlining what you can do to it). This is the legal document for the sale, which you need to read carefully before signing a contract to purchase the property. The person selling the property is responsible for providing the statement, and it is typically prepared for them by a legal representative.

Once you've read the section 32 and done your due diligence, you decide if you're going to make an offer or not. The kind of due diligence you'll need to do will depend on the property type and location. For example, if you're looking at a rural location, you'll need to consider things such as flood and fire risk, which can have an impact on your insurance premiums and potentially restrict your capacity to renovate or extend.

You'll also receive a title document. It's a good idea to compare the measurements on that document with what you see at the site to ensure the boundaries depicted are accurate. On the Mordialloc title there were four car-parking spots at the back of the block. I found out later that one isn't big enough for anything larger than a bumper car. Fortunately, my park was just big enough for my little hatchback. I should have checked this properly beforehand.

If you're planning to renovate or build, it's essential to review the local planning scheme as there may be restrictions, such as heritage overlays, that prevent you from achieving your vision. It's also worth checking in with the local council to see what's going on in the area. If there are planned developments, like a massive block of apartments due to be erected nearby, you'll want to know about that in advance.

In my case, the main issue was understanding the owners corporation and its associated finances. I needed to be clear on what was in the budget, what works, if any, were planned, and I'd have enough in the bank in case emergency repairs were required.

If you're purchasing someone else's existing investment property, there is likely to be a lease attached. The tenant may be on a twelve-month lease or be paying month to month. You need to know how long they'll continue living in the property before you can access it. If it's a twelve-month lease, you have to wait for their lease to finish, but if they're leasing month to month then you or the tenant can give notice after settlement, in line with the lease's requirements.

The body corporate figures were in reasonable shape and there was a tenant on a month-to-month agreement. That worked for me, as it gave me more time to stay with my folks before moving in. Now all I had to do was pay a visit to the bank and see if they were up for handing over hundreds of thousands of dollars so I could buy it. I'd have to dig out some serious grown-up clothes for that meeting.

First-homeowner incentives

Incentives for first home buyers aren't new. Governments have been dishing out cash and discounts to those trying to enter the market since 1964. Yep, even our folks had sneaky ways into the market.

But it's not always the help it appears to be. Yes, with a first-homebuyer's grant you get a leg-up onto the property ladder, but the grant itself plays a role in maintaining property values more broadly, protecting those who are already in the market. Yes, it helps individuals, but it's a larger-scale intervention that can work to keep demand steady and therefore protect the market from declines. For example, in 2019, in Australian states where the market had slumped such as Sydney and Melbourne, first-homebuyer activity remained consistent due to these incentives and exemptions of stamp duty. Of course, you're not going to turn down these benefits if you're trying to buy and they fit with your vision, just don't let stimulant of the moment dictate what you purchase. Regional first-homebuyer bonuses are often excellent, but do you really want to set up a new life out of the city? It's a big decision.

Back when I was looking, I was eligible for a first-homeowners grant of $7000 if I bought a new place. But for me, as we already know, a brand-new off-the-plan property was going to be prohibitively expensive, even with the $7000 saving. I could get something much more affordable if I bought an older home, and I wouldn't be paying extortionate owners corporation fees for shiny lifts and swimming pools.

Stamp duty

Stamp duty is a retro term. Essentially, property buyers pay for the government to 'rubber stamp' their purchase – at the core, it's just a hefty administration fee. Most people resent paying stamp duty – understandably – because it's a huge expense. The government makes a stack out of it.

But there are other reasons for it. One advantage of stamp duty is that it makes it harder to buy and sell properties: because there are stamp duty requirements attached to every purchase, it reduces the ease with which people collect investments or flip homes for a quick profit. Stamp duty costs must be factored into every purchase. So, in theory, it levels the playing field, ensuring that investors can't completely outrun aspiring owner-occupiers.

At that time, as a first home buyer, if I purchased an existing property I was eligible for a 40 per cent reduction in stamp duty. That saved me about $5000. By 2017, Victoria completely abolished stamp duty for first home buyers purchasing homes worth up to $600,000 and applied a concession for properties priced between $600,000 and $750,000.

The first-homebuyer concessions vary from state to state and they change frequently. Currently, in Victoria, it's $10,000 when you buy or build a new home worth up to $750,000. In some places, like regional Victoria, it's more: $20,000 if you're prepared to get out of town. In Sydney, they're now offering a stamp-duty exemption on new homes worth up to $650,000 and land that costs up to $350,000. There's also a concession for existing properties worth between $650,000 and $800,000 and land valued between $350,000 and $450,000.

Stamp duty is still a massive hurdle for first home buyers in some states. In Adelaide, for example, there are no stamp duty exemptions, but some buyers might be eligible for off-the-plan concessions. In Tasmania, there are no stamp duty exemptions but, from July 2019, the first-homebuyers grant is $10,000. To check out the stamp duty requirements in your location, visit your state government website.

To be eligible for the 40 per cent stamp duty reduction in Victoria, I had to move into my property within the first twelve months. If there was an existing rental tenant when I purchased, time was allowed for them to complete their lease. Once they moved out, I'd have to live there for at least a year to confirm it was my principal residence – so I needed to be sure I'd be comfortable living on my own in Mordialloc for a stint.

Lender's mortgage insurance

I can't believe I didn't know about lender's mortgage insurance (LMI) until I was buying my home. That 20 per cent deposit felt like the biggest barrier to entering the market. The fact is, you don't always need 20 per cent. Seriously, we think we need $130,000 in the bank to buy a $650,000 home? It's no wonder we're all like 'yeah, nah'. The thing is, that's not necessarily the case. Let me give you a run-down.

LMI is a fee banks and lenders change the borrower when their purchase is risky – usually when the deposit is less than 20 per cent. You'll technically pay the lump sum when you settle the property, but often it's built into your loan and added to your mortgage repayments. You don't need the money upfront (which is handy because that's why you're considering LMI in the first place).

LMI gets mixed reviews because it's an additional cost in the long term when added to your loan, and it's risky because you're buying with less than 20 per cent, using insurance to protect the risk. But, because the cost of LMI can be built into your mortgage and spread over the life of the loan, it becomes a tiny amount of your monthly mortgage payment. Although it attracts interest when it's added to your loan, LMI is tax-deductible for the first five years if it's taken out on the purchase of an investment property. Plus, if you can bargain the asking price of your property down, you effectively cancel out the cost of the LMI.

In my case, the purchase price I intended to offer was lower than what the vendor wanted and using LMI got me into the market twelve months faster than it would have if I'd waited to save the entire 20 per cent. Another year later, the purchase price was much higher than I'd paid, so I would have needed to save even more to reach a 20 per cent deposit. Plus, I'd reached a year with my folks and faced a return to renting, which would have meant another $12,000 or so spent on someone else's investment property. No thank you.

Another example: if you are considering using LMI and you seek to buy a $500,000 home with a $70,000, 14 per cent deposit, your estimated LMI cost could be as little as $5000, depending on your provider. So, your $430,000 mortgage becomes a $435,000 mortgage.

And, in the event that your property value rises $100,000, the cost of your LMI is effectively absorbed by the rise in value.

If you'd waited to save a $100,000 deposit, the property might be worth $550,000 and that means you'll still only have 18 per cent. Had you bought it at $500,000 using LMI, you'd be ahead financially compared to someone who waited to buy with a higher deposit.

In a slowing market, you mightn't need LMI. If prices are stabilising or dropping, you have the luxury of taking the time to save more. That said, mortgage broker Ben Ong suggests it can still be worth drawing on the premium if it helps you to achieve your goal: 'If it's a property people are planning on living in for a long time and it's a one-off they can't see anywhere else, they could use it.' LMI would enable a buyer to nab that property then and there. If you miss out on a property you really love and want to call home simply because you didn't have a 20 per cent deposit, that could be disappointing, and LMI might prevent that.

But, like I said, for LMI to be worth it, your property should be a long-term investment. In an unstable market, you may be better off waiting until you have a larger deposit, which reduces your risk and the risk the bank takes, too. The bigger your deposit, the lower your risk. Here's why.

If I buy a home for $300,000 using a 10 per cent deposit and LMI, I've only paid for 10 per cent of what I owe. If, however, I buy it with a 30 per cent deposit, I've paid almost a third of what I owe. If the market dips 10 per cent and I've only paid off 10 per cent, things become risky if I have to sell. But if I've paid off 30 per cent and the market dips by 10 per cent, I'm still in front – if I have to sell, it's unlikely that I wouldn't get more than I owe.

How is LMI calculated?

The amount of LMI you'll pay will depend on a number of factors including the purchase price and the amount of risk you're taking.

At any price point, LMI will also vary from lender to lender, but as a general rule the percentage rises with two factors: the greater the cost of the home, and the lower the deposit. Here are a couple of examples of how LMI is calculated.

A $300,000 property purchased with a 15 per cent deposit will have an LMI premium of about 0.7 per cent added to the loan. This figure rises to about 1.1 per cent if the property is priced between $500,000 and $600,000, but also with a 15 per cent deposit. If you want the $300,000 property but you only have a 10 per cent deposit, your LMI could be approximately 1.4 per cent. In the case of the more expensive property, priced between $500,000 and $600,000, and purchased with a 10 per cent deposit, the LMI premium will be closer to 2.1 per cent.

These figures are a rough guide. You can use online LMI calculators to get an idea of how this might operate for the property you're looking at and the size of the deposit you're hoping to put up. But the only way to be certain of the LMI premium you're up for is by talking to your mortgage broker or lender about the precise figure.

Loan-to-value ratio

You want to avoid selling your property for less than the loan-value at all costs – that means you don't want to sell for less than you owe the lender. If you've paid a 20 per cent deposit and owned a property for a few years, your loan-to-value ratio should protect you from selling at a loss. Here's a really simple example.

If the property you want to buy is worth $500,000 and you have a 20 per cent – $100,000 – deposit, you will need a loan of $400,000. In other words, because you can afford 20 per cent of the value, your loan-to-value ratio is 80 per cent. Your property's value would have to dip by more than 20 per cent for you to risk selling at a loss, which means you're in a reasonably safe position.

When you use LMI, you push your loan-to-value ratio up, and therefore take on more risk. If you only have a 5 per cent deposit and the value dips by 7 per cent, your property is worth less than you paid. According to Ben Ong, most lenders will allow the loan-to-value ratio to run up to 95 per cent for owner-occupiers seeking to buy, including LMI. 'But for investment properties there are very few lenders that would run above 90 per cent, with some stopping at 80 per cent,' he explains.

Essentially, the size of the deposit required and the amount of LMI the lender provides will depend on several factors, including whether your preferred property is in the city or a remote location. If it's an apartment that's less than 50 or 60 square metres of internal living space or a rural spot, they may want to keep the loan-to-value ratio at 80 per cent or below, meaning you'll need that 20 per cent deposit. As an owner-occupier purchasing an apartment that was well over 60 square metres in a suburb that wasn't at risk of oversupply, I understood that I wouldn't necessarily need a 20 per cent deposit.

Banks have tightened their lending criteria since the 2018 banking royal commission. The aim of the inquiry was to assess misconduct across the banking, superannuation and financial services industries. During the hearings, over-lending in the consumer home loans market was heavily scrutinised, and, as a result, more comprehensive assessment of applications is now occurring. While this might feel like yet another hurdle for homebuyers seeking loans, it should result in banks providing responsible service that enables you to get a loan you can manage.

The assessment criteria continue to evolve. This is where it can really help to talk to a mortgage broker. Particularly if you're not a numbers person, they can help translate some of these complexities so you understand exactly how much you need before you prepare to apply for your loan.

Getting the loan

Once you know what type of dwelling you're interested in, in which suburb, and you have an idea of how large a deposit you can get together, you can start to more accurately calculate how much a lender will provide and what your out-of-pocket costs will be in total. Here are the steps I took.

1. Estimate your purchase price

We picked a range of possible purchase prices between $300,000 and $350,000 and developed budgets for all of the scenarios. This helped me to see what the cost differences would be between a property purchase of, say, $310,000, versus one at $340,000. Let's crunch the numbers based on a sale price of $350,000

2. Work out your maximum loan-to-value ratio

Your loan-to-value ratio is the percentage of the loan funded by the bank. The remaining amount is the deposit you put up yourself. If your loan-to-value ratio is 80 per cent, the remaining 20 per cent will come from your savings.

For a $350,000 property with a loan-to-value ratio of 80 per cent, the total loan amount is $280,000. Your deposit will be $70,000.

3. Establish the loan components for purchase

If you're in the position to put up a 20 per cent deposit – or more – your loan may only be for the remaining amount. In my case, my deposit was only 10 per cent, so I would be needing to invest in (and pay for) LMI. The total I owed would include the loan, plus the LMI.

For a $350,000 property, with a loan of 90 per cent (using a 10 per cent deposit of $35,000), the LMI would be approximately $6240 (calculated at a premium of 1.78 per cent), depending on the loan lender. The LMI amount is added to the total loan-to-value ratio, bringing the loan total to 91.78 per cent. At 91.78 per cent, that makes the loan amount for my $350,000 property come to a total of $321,230. Here's the breakdown:

Purchase price: $350,000

Deposit: $35,000 (10 per cent)

Loan amount (90 per cent): $315,000

LMI (1.78 per cent): $6240

Total: $321,230 (a loan of 91.78 per cent)

4. Estimate your total additional settlement costs

Your additional costs will vary, depending on your circumstances and the time of purchase. Not only will the bank want to see that you have the deposit funds, they'll also want proof that you can cover all additional settlement costs when you apply for the loan. Here's an example of the additional costs I was up for.

Government charges (stamp duty): $7189

Estimated finance fees: $500

Legal conveyancing fees: $1320

Planning and title searches: $275

Updated owner's corporation certificate: $0 (not required)

Registration of caveat on property: $253

Loan application and other costs: $375

Total additional costs: $9912

Stamp duty is the big one here. If I'd been buying now, in 2019, my out-of-pocket costs would have been vastly less – about $2723 – because I wouldn't have been up for stamp duty. That's life, though.

5. Summarise your deposit and additional costs

....

Deposit: $35,000

Additional costs: $9912

....

Total: $44,912

....

6. Estimate your monthly mortgage repayments

At the time, we calculated my monthly repayments based on a thirty-year mortgage with interest rates of 5.08 per cent, to allow for possible rate rises. You can use one of the bank's mortgage calculators and plug in your estimated loan amount and interest.

My estimated monthly repayments came to $1700.

After digesting the digits in that example, I quickly understood that $350,000 was outside my budget at this point. I didn't have $44,000. So I either had to find something more affordable, use an even smaller deposit with LMI or wait longer.

The upside was that I'd only need the deposit when I agreed to make the purchase at the time I was applying for the loan. I would have to hustle again to find the money for the additional costs at settlement. This is probably not something you could do now; you might need to have all settlement funds available when you apply for the loan. But at the time, if I bought a $300,000 property with a 9 per cent deposit, I needed about $27,000 when I signed the contract and another $9000 when it came time to settle. I would need $36,000 and I had less than $30,000 at this point. So, I knew I needed a long settlement. Ideally ninety days. Working to numbers like this was doable.

After working out my maximum loan – which included the cost of the loan itself, the cost of LMI, stamp duty, legal fees, authority costs (any costs associated with the title) and registration of a caveat, which meant that no one could negotiate on the property while I did – I was ready to present my case to the bank.

What kind of loan is best?

When you're paying off a home loan, it's important to understand that there is interest on the loan as well as the principal. Say you borrow $300,000 to purchase the property, that amount – $300,000 – is the principal, and the bank will charge you interest on it. When it comes to choosing a loan, you can select one in which you pay the interest *and* the principal simultaneously, or you can arrange to pay interest only for the first few years.

Principal+interest loans

With a principal+interest loan, you're paying down your principal – the actual loan – from the get-go. In the early days, though, you'll probably be paying more interest than principal. The banks are clever like that. I remember my first payment coming out of my account and I was like 'What the hell . . . ?' It was mostly interest. It felt like it took a year just to own the front door.

The advantage of choosing a principal+interest loan is that the interest rate will generally be lower than it is on an interest-only loan. Mortgage broker Ben Ong gives the example of a principal+interest loan for a $300,000 home with an interest rate of 3.78 per cent, compared to a 4.13 per cent rate for interest-only. The numbers add up.

In addition to the lower interest rate, the benefit of principal+interest is that you're paying down the actual loan, rather than just tackling the interest. Paying down your principal, however gradually, can protect you from price drops. Let's say, for example, you've managed to pay down $100,000 of a $300,000 loan, while also tackling the interest as required. If you then had to sell for $280,000, at least you're in front. By contrast, when you're paying interest-only, you're not paying back any of what you owe, so you're relying on the value of the property to go up to protect you in the case of potentially needing to sell.

Interest-only loans

Interest-only loans last for about five years, during which time you're only paying the interest. The principal stays as it was. People do this because it makes their repayments lower, but only for the interest-only period. Once that's over, you switch to a principal+interest loan anyway, at which point your repayments go up significantly, to compensate for the fact that you hadn't been paying your principal. The interest rate will generally be higher than it would be on a principal+interest loan, too.

Why would people do this? Good question. The answer might be to do with life circumstances at the time of purchase. If you're buying a home and planning to have a baby, for example, the lower repayments could enable one partner to manage the mortgage on their own while the other works as a primary carer. When the primary carer is back at work, it's easier to tackle the higher principal+interest repayments on two incomes.

According to Ben, interest-only loans are still widely available, despite the general tightening of lending. 'Banks typically want a justification,' he explains. One party being on maternity leave is an example of this. 'The crucial difference now is that on a thirty-year loan with a five-year interest-only period, banks will assess the servicing capability on the remaining P&I [principle + interest] period of twenty-five years,' he says. That means the bank needs to be confident that you can cover the hike in the repayments when the time comes, even though it's years away.

If we take the example of a lender offering interest-only loans of 4.13 per cent on a property purchased by an owner-occupier for $300,000, repayments will look something like $1033 per month for the first five years. Then they blow out – quite significantly – to $1606 when the interest-only period comes to an end.

'Before tighter lending, banks would want to see you could repay $1033 and didn't worry about when the interest-only period finished, so some people would just refinance again to another interest-only loan at the end of the five-year period, never paying down the loan, counting on their property growing in value,' Ben explains. Things have shifted since the global financial crisis, however. Now, lenders will want to see that you can afford the remaining twenty-five years of payments at $1606. They might also test your capacity to service the loan if interest rates were to rise to 8 per cent, for example. 'In real terms they want to see if the borrower can afford monthly payments of up to $2315,' he says.

If you need to sell and you've only paid interest for a few years, you still owe the entire principal amount. In that case, if for some miraculous reason your property doubled in value in a few years, you'd be sweet. But if the market didn't move much in your purchase area, you potentially walk away with nothing once you've paid out the loan.

Fixed versus variable interest rates

If you reckon that interest rates are going to go through the roof, you might negotiate to have a fixed-interest rate applied to part, or all, of your loan. But, like interest-only loans, there are ways that you might pay later for the security of paying less interest if rates do indeed go up. For example, your fixed-interest rate might be higher than a variable-interest rate when interest rates are low. In other words, you're paying more for the privilege of knowing that the interest rate doesn't move, as it will for other borrowers. You may also face financial penalties if you want to get out of a fixed-interest scenario.

Loan pre-approval

Once I'd spoken to the bank and filled in a bunch of forms detailing the specifics of my financial position, I received conditional pre-approval for a loan. This doesn't last forever. For me it was three months.

If I didn't get Mordialloc, I'd have to make an offer on something else in that time frame. If it lapsed, I'd have to apply again.

With pre-approval signed off, I was able to tell the real estate agent I would be able to secure a loan and make an actual offer. But I was under no obligation to proceed just yet. During this time, the vendor didn't have to accept an offer that was 'conditional'. When you make an offer and sign a contract that's conditional, it means things are still yet to happen before it becomes *un*conditional and you and the vendor are proceeding to settlement. Conditions you may request include a building inspection. Or, as in my case, the bank might want to send their own valuation expert to the property, to ensure that what you're offering is in line with what they think it's worth. Once they'd done this and the bank was satisfied that my offer matched their valuation, I was in a position to tell my lawyer that approval was confirmed, and that he could, at that point, inform the vendor's representative that the contract was unconditional. In other words, we were good to go.

At this point, I was officially moving forward to settlement, which happens within a period agreed to by both the vendor and the purchaser. For me, that period was ninety days. Shit was officially getting real.

Using LMI (and other tricks) to get into the market faster

Savvy millennials are factoring LMI into their property purchase plans while they're saving, so the dream feels achievable early in the process. Twenty-five-year-old paralegal Zarah Tenorino, and her partner, 27-year-old mental health support worker Bryan, set a deposit target of 5 per cent, rather than aiming for 20 per cent. The Darwin-based couple started their power-save with a simple philosophy. 'We just stopped spending money on unnecessary things. We stopped eating out every night and haven't had a major holiday overseas,' Zarah says matter-of-factly.

'I never thought I should worry about buying before thirty,' she adds. But a bit of research changed that. Now, she says, 'I am rushing to get into the property market and stop paying someone else's mortgage.'

Zarah, who's originally from the Philippines, has Australian permanent residency, but isn't entitled to HECS to cover her law degree. 'This year I paid almost $10,000 in university costs upfront, which could've easily been used for a house deposit,' she says.

To maintain their motivation, Zarah and Bryan spent all of 2018 looking at properties. Despite their demanding schedules, they wanted to know the market inside out and understand exactly what they could get for their hard-earned coin. Thorough research would also give them a clear idea of their preferences – what they did and didn't want in a home.

They found out about the potential benefits of LMI thanks to their mortgage broker, and set their sights on a home and land package worth somewhere between $550,000 and $560,000. 'We are hoping not to go over $600,000, including ancillary costs such as reports, tests and legal costs,' Zarah told me before they started looking. At first, they considered existing houses, but 'we could always find a fault,' she says. So they began to look at new build options. In November 2018 they settled on a package in the relatively new Darwin suburb of Zuccoli, paying $230,000 for land and agreeing to a $340,000 home with four bedrooms, a media room, two bathrooms and a garage.

Between them, they'd saved $40,000 and also received a $26,000 first-homebuyers' grant. They still needed $23,000 in LMI to make up the deposit for a total loan of approximately $600,000. They're not concerned about using LMI. 'The amount we would've paid in rent if we had waited until we had 20 per cent would have cost us more, and house prices may have gone up in that time due to the removal of fracking restrictions here in the Northern Territory,' Zarah explains. Plus, it makes more financial sense to be in the market. They were spending $390 per week on rent while they saved. 'We are not scared of mortgage repayments or LMI, because we'd rather have that $390 per week in our own property.'

They plan to live in it for at least five years, but the long-term dream is ambitious. 'We want our dream home and probably another property for my parents. They are in a very bad position financially, so I want to get a home loan approved, let them live in it while they pay rent and give them the house once the mortgage is over,' Zarah says. While it would be nice to have a property portfolio, they're not planning to overextend themselves: they're equally focused on excelling in their careers, not just 'having a property side hustle'.

They moved into their property in mid-2019 with their three-year-old daughter. Finally, they're able to enjoy life in a new home that's designed exactly the way they envisioned. They say the LMI, which is built into the cost of their loan, is a small price to pay for the security of having their own place.

Avos of wisdom

 If you're eligible, make sure you understand what the first-homebuyers' benefits are in your state, and whether they work for your circumstances and the property you want.

 Work with a mortgage broker or finance expert to be clear on what you'll owe when you sign the contract and settle the property, so there are no unexpected expenses.

 Remember, pre-approval doesn't last forever. Make sure you know how long you've got.

 When selecting a loan type, think about what makes the most sense not just now, but in the future.

9

Signing Off on the Biggest Debt of My Life

IT WAS MID-FEBRUARY IN 2014 and we'd finally settled on a price. Three hundred and twelve thousand dollars. This was $8000 less than the original asking price. The finance had been approved and I'd provided a verbal agreement to proceed with the sale. It was happening.

At that time I was still working at the PR agency, taking a day each week to write freelance features. I was sitting at my desk at home, happily drafting an article, when my boss's name flashed up on my phone ... which was weird. She never called me on my day off.

'Nic,' she said. I knew it was bad news the moment she spoke. 'I really hate to have to tell you this, but we're making some changes and unfortunately your role is going to come to an end.'

This was not in the plan.

I was gracious. She was apologetic. I'd have a few more days to wrap up the project I was working on and then, well, that was it: core income stream cancelled.

I called Dad, dropped a series of expletives and then even he, who'd encouraged me wholeheartedly from the beginning of the process, expressed caution: it was going to be really important to think carefully about this now. I could finalise the sale. I had the money for the deposit, but then I would have to work out where the hell I was going to get enough to fund everything that came next.

I battled mixed emotions: exhilaration at being a buyer at last and terror of the commitment. What if I screwed up and was lumped with hundreds of thousands of dollars of debt I couldn't manage? It'd make dealing with the credit card debt feel comparatively breezy.

I had a gut feeling, though, that this was a reasonably safe bet. It was a good property in a growing area and the price was competitive. I had to take the risk and secure it. But I also needed a new job immediately if I was going to save the extra amount I needed to cover the additional costs at settlement.

What happens if property prices drop after you buy?

Taking a risk can be a costly exercise. Nicole, thirty-five, met her husband Nathaniel, forty, when she was nineteen. Before they started to save for a home, they cleared the debt they'd accrued on cars and whitegoods. They started saving for their deposit about a year and a half before they were ready to apply for a loan.

In July 2008, they bought a two-bedroom cottage in the Bundaberg suburb of Svensson Heights for $208,000. It has a lock-up garage, a shed and a large garden. Securing their home felt like a massive win, but two and a half years later, in December 2011, a devastating flood swept through Queensland. Homes were uninhabitable, rescue services used small motorboats to get around the streets, and people waded through waist-deep water to collect their belongings.

In 2013, just as Bundaberg was recovering, floods happened again. Nicole and Nathaniel's home was saved on both occasions because

Svensson Heights, as the name implies, is elevated. But while their suburb was never under direct threat, the devastation had a ripple effect. More than five years later, Nicole says, 'The town is hurting. People are very scared of anything new and many older stores are closing due to ever-increasing costs.'

After this part of Queensland dried out, many people were left without their homes, which meant a lot of residents had to rent. In fact, so many people needed temporary accommodation that Nicole says some of her neighbours subdivided their properties and added additional dwellings to capitalise on the sudden and dramatic demand for rentals. So, while property prices dropped, demand for rentals was high and remains high today. 'You can buy a crappy three-bedroom house for $245,000 and rent it out for $280 a week,' Nicole adds.

It's hard to say why demand for rentals has remained high, but Nicole believes a growing population has played a part. 'I know a lot of tradies left the Gladstone mine and moved here when it started downsizing in 2016–17, that may also be a part of it,' she muses. There's also an ageing population of people who are set in their ways. 'They don't seem to care that the younger generation want modern shops and interesting things to do,' she says. Nicole and Nathaniel are doing their bit for Bundaberg's next generation – they run a martial arts training school, giving kids an opportunity to exercise and socialise.

Property values still haven't completely bounced back almost a decade later. Cruise through Bundaberg listings on real estate websites and you'll find a range of homes listed for between $200,000 and $230,000. We can learn something from this: property markets are different from state to state. Growth has not been consistent across the country. The quirks and specifics of local economies have a big impact on prices.

'Our house, with $40,000 worth of renovations and solar power, is still worth $30,000 less than we bought it for,' Nicole laments. But instead of freaking out or selling, Nicole and Nathaniel have worked hard to pay off their mortgage so they're debt-free. In November 2018, they achieved that goal, knocking over the entire debt in just over a decade. 'We always paid more than our minimum repayment, and for every pay rise I got, 80 per cent went on the mortgage and 20 per cent went to the rising cost of living.'

But it's been a slog. Nicole clocked up forty hours each week as a supply manager for local and rural hospitals and, on top of that, thirty hours a week in the family business. They're raising their eight-year-old daughter, too. But once the mortgage was paid off, Nicole left her job to focus on the family's martial arts school.

'We intend to live here for another seven years while we save for our dream home, so we haven't really lost the money. You only lose when you sell,' Nicole points out. 'It will make a great rental, and all the houses with land in the neighbourhood are being subdivided, so over time our house will bounce back,' she adds. They've replaced the roof and repaired ceilings and walls, fixing a mould problem that was overlooked by a building inspector prior to purchase. They've painted and added solar panels. In time, the couple may consider lifting the house and putting two additional bedrooms and an extra living room downstairs, further adding to the appeal. With all the local subdivisions, they'll have 'the only house in the street with a big yard'.

Although their experience has been less than ideal, they have the right attitude. Property prices will rise and fall, but theirs is a long-term investment. 'It's been tough, but I wouldn't change it for the world,' Nicole says.

The costs of selling

Agent's fees

The most obvious cost to a vendor is the agent's fees. Agents charge a commission that is payable when the house sells. These figures vary nationally, but let's use a typical example of 2 per cent. If your house sells for $550,000, and the agent's fee is 2 per cent, that's $11,000 straight to the agent. The agent's marketing campaign, ensuring your property is listed on the major property websites as well as featured in advertisements, is an additional cost. The cost of the campaign will depend on the type of home and its value. If you're reading a glossy property lift-out in the weekend papers and see a full-page ad for a multimillion-dollar home, the vendor has paid for that. Let's say your marketing campaign costs $2000 on top of the agent's fees.

Staging costs

If you don't reside in a home full of art and designer furniture, you may also consider having your home 'staged'. This means you'll move some or all of your furniture out and replace it with rental furniture for the duration of the campaign. It's becoming increasingly popular to pay a professional to bring in everything from lamps to artwork. They'll even replace the bedding so your rooms look flawless. But again, you're going to pay for this. The stager's fee will depend on how much they're bringing into your home and how long the campaign goes for. You could easily pay anywhere from $2000 to $10,000, or even more. It's a lot to spend, but having your home immaculately presented can make a huge difference to the final price tag. Let's say staging costs you $5000.

You've now paid $11,000 in commission to your agent, $2000 for marketing and $5000 for staging. When your home sells for $550,000, you actually walk away with $532,000.

Discharge request fees

You're up for a couple of hundred dollars in administration fees just to end your home loan. This will vary from bank to bank, but it could be about $500.

131

Break fees

If you arranged a fixed interest rate, you'll probably also have to pay a break fee to your lender. This is an amount charged when you pay off a loan before the contracted term is complete, to cover the loss of any further profit the lender would have achieved over the duration.

Conveyancing fees

A conveyancer or lawyer will manage the settlement of your property in the same way they did when you bought it. They'll work with the bank to ensure the change in ownership is managed correctly. Fees vary, but expect to pay approximately $1000.

Capital gains tax

You'll either make a capital gain or a capital loss when you sell a property. I'd heard the names of these dreaded taxes bandied about, but until I got into the property game I didn't know what they were. They apply, I learned, when your property is an investment. If it's your principal residence, you typically won't have to pay capital gains, but for investors who've made a gain, the profit on the sale is counted as additional income, which is taxable. When tax time rolls around, you'll need to declare that extra income in your return.

Here's a sense of how it works: if you bought a place for $550,000 and sold it for $650,000, then you made $100,000. That 'income' is added to the money you've made through your salary. It's kind of like having a second job. When you have a second job, you're usually taxed at 50 per cent, so any capital gain you make will also be taxed at 50 per cent. But while your boss, if you have one, most likely withholds tax from your salary over the course of the year, so you don't owe a lump sum at tax time, that's not the case with property. You'll need to be prepared to pay up, because your taxable income will be higher. That's why it's good to talk to your mortgage broker or use a capital

gains tax calculator to get a sense of what you might owe. (You're lia-
ble for capital gains tax when you sign a contract with the buyer, not
when the property is settled. So, if you sign the paperwork in May,
you'll have to record the capital gain for that financial year when you
do your tax return in July, even if the property doesn't settle until the
new financial year.)

What happens in the lead-up to settlement

Fortunately, my role in the PR agency wasn't ending because I was
underperforming. My boss gave me a glowing recommendation to
an advertising agency called The Royals, just around the corner from
where I'd been working. I met with their strategy director, Dave,
who told me that there was an opportunity to work as a social media
manager for a range of their clients. The office, on the third floor of
a historic Richmond building, stands out thanks to its iconic roof-
mounted sign advertising Slade Knitwear in huge cursive letters.
I didn't know when I sat down opposite Dave that the space would
become my second home.

I fielded questions casually and he seemed to think I'd be a good
fit. It took all my strength not to beg. *Please give me this job, I've just
bought an apartment I really can't afford.* I wasn't exactly passionate
about writing social media posts for brands, but whatever. I'd do it
for a year and look for something better aligned with my career goals in
the meantime. In my previous role, I'd been earning more than $4000
per month working a four-day week, leaving me time to make some
extra cash as a freelancer. Now I'd be earning a bit over $4000 per
month, but working a five-day week, meaning less time to freelance.
But I wasn't in a position to be choosy. The position meant accepting
a reduction in income if I couldn't keep up the freelance work, and a
slight career detour, but honestly, I would've accepted a role cleaning toilets if that's what he'd offered. I needed this gig immediately.

I'd just have to make it work. I signed the contract the moment it landed in my hand and I saved everything I could in the first three months to make sure I had the settlement funds.

Settlement is the legal process that wraps up the sale and makes the transfer of ownership from the vendor to the purchaser official. The key players involved in the settlement process include: you, your bank, your mortgage broker (if you have one), your legal representative and the seller's financial and legal people.

Essentially, there'll be a heap of emails back and forth between your conveyancer or solicitor and mortgage broker, whoever is managing the settlement process, and the vendor's equivalents. It's your job to read these emails carefully, make absolutely certain that the numbers are correct, and then to confirm that you've got the cash in the bank as agreed. Your solicitor or conveyancer will ensure the vendor's existing mortgage is closed and will crosscheck with the vendor's representative to make sure all clauses have been completed. Finally, they'll make sure the transfer of land and the mortgage that is moving into your name are correctly registered with the relevant government bodies in your state.

A few days before my settlement was due to take place, in May 2014, I got an email from my lawyer confirming the loan amount that the bank would supply as well as the figure they would draw from my account. The deposit had already been taken from my account and the bank had added the lender's mortgage insurance to the cost of the loan when I agreed to the contract.

All up, I needed another $7000 in my account to cover the additional charges. I'd managed to save this in the three months since I'd paid my deposit, but when those funds came out, I'd be back to almost zero again. I had a bit more time up my sleeve to pay my lawyer for his work – another $1300.

The final figure was adjusted, to allow for rates that had been paid and rent paid by the tenant currently in the property. Prior to settlement, I also had the right to a final inspection of the apartment to ensure it was in the same condition as when I signed the contract some months earlier.

Now the bank would provide the remaining loan funds and I was up for the stamp duty, minus a 40 per cent discount thanks to my first-homebuyer concession. To get this figure correct, I had to sign yet more paperwork confirming I was eligible. I also had to cover the cost of the titles office transfer fee and titles office mortgage registration fee. The bank advised my lawyer that they would draw the remaining funds from my account on settlement – that's the stamp duty and other costs accounted for on my spreadsheet.

Becoming a homeowner

I logged into internet banking on settlement afternoon to see that the process was complete. One moment all my remaining savings were sitting there, the next my mortgage offset account appeared below my savings account and my credit card account. I had about $17 to my name and a new mortgage account with a balance of approximately *minus* $300,000. Ouch.

Just like that, I was a homeowner.

Nothing changed immediately. The tenant living in my apartment on a month-to-month lease was happy to stay. This meant his rent covered most of the mortgage, initially. When the first payment came out of my account, I only needed to add a few hundred dollars to cover the gap. I knew I had an obligation to move in within the first twelve months, in accordance with the first-homebuyer benefit – the 40 per cent reduction in stamp duty I'd received (which was deducted during the settlement process, although the way stamp duty is paid can vary depending on your location and the loan arrangements). There was some precious time to get some reserve funds into the bank before I moved in. Once again, I switched on the power-save button. I hoped to have a couple of mortgage repayments saved before I moved in, so it was back to high-velocity budgeting.

Getting my head around a new role was enough of a challenge without the demands of extra freelance work, so I killed off the side projects. My annual salary was less than I'd been bringing in while consulting and writing articles, but still, if I continued to live on the shoestring allowance I'd become accustomed to, it'd be fine – right? I hoped so.

It didn't take long to love The Royals. In fact, within the first few months I began wondering, *What's the catch?* I was paid to show up every day at a playground for grown-ups. Although the work could be demanding, I had access to all the coffee I could drink, which was invaluable on my budget. I couldn't afford the unofficial uniform – staff were rocking skinny jeans, white t-shirts and leather jackets, tattoos optional – as I was still surviving on discarded samples from a fast-fashion chain store my brother's girlfriend worked at. Fortunately, my colleagues seemed to find my synthetic floral prints refreshing. The meeting rooms were named after celebrities who'd been arrested. Regular pub lunches often carried on for hours. Every staff member had access to the music via the wifi, and we queued songs to ensure there was a nonstop soundtrack running through the open-plan working space. Come 4 pm on a Friday, the volume rose, corks were popped, and the weekend was ushered in. A Mexican wave of laptops folded and we would retire to the windows that overlooked the city, play card games and trade stories until well after dark.

On these nights, I'd forget the weight of responsibility that I'd committed to. I was a regular 31-year-old with a stable job and awesome colleagues who were becoming my friends. The capacity to free-pour wine without worrying about what it was costing was positively restorative. I quickly became the self-appointed 'head of culture', forcing my party playlists on the team and habitually dialling up my Friday night energy so people would stay. There's no need to head to a bar when you can perform karaoke in the office till midnight. Considering I'd accepted this job in a moment of desperation, I'd really landed on my feet.

But when my tenant gave notice of his intended exit a month later, I was jolted back to reality. I'd put away a few thousand dollars, but in four weeks' time I would have to pay to move, start covering the whole mortgage on my own – about $1550 per month – and pay a round of owners corporation fees, too. I was terrified.

I'd calculated already that each month, once I'd paid my mortgage, bought food, paid bills (including my ever-demanding credit cards) and covered my car payments, I'd be lucky if I was left with about $100 per week in the bank. I'd become pretty accustomed to living lean, but the stakes had been lower, living at my folks' house with the security of their roof over my head. If I needed to dip into my savings for an unexpected expense, I could. Now, I had very little saved for emergencies and I absolutely could not miss a mortgage repayment. I knew that for the foreseeable future I'd be walking a financial tightrope with no safety net to fall into.

Avos of wisdom

 Property prices will rise and fall over time. Nicole and Nathan's story shows that even if property prices don't spike in your area, paying off your mortgage gives you an asset.

 If you later think you want to sell, make sure you're aware of all the associated costs. If you're investing, capital gains tax could absorb a big chunk of your profits.

 Settlement can be overhwhelming, but you *must* read all the documents and check the figures. No one cares about getting it right more than you do.

 Ensure you're as prepared as possible for settlement and aim to have additional funds ready for moving, bills, unanticipated expenses and that all-important first mortgage repayment.

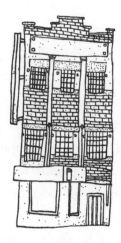

10

The First Year
(The Shit Bit)

THE REMOVALISTS ARRIVED EARLY ON a crisp Saturday
morning in late June. Boxes that hadn't been opened since I lived in
the rat house with Beck were thrown in with the handful of boxes I
had been living out of during my time with my folks. When the last of
my bedroom furniture was in the truck, I got in the car and drove
to my new home, my parents convoying behind.

Once I found the champagne flutes, we opened the bottle the agent
had supplied and I toasted my parents for putting me up while I saved.
I suspected they were toasting the fact that I was finally moving out.
I was happy to be resuming my adult life, but I knew it would take some
adjustment. I had become accustomed to eating with my family at the
end of the day, and to always having someone to talk to. I never said it
out loud, but I knew I'd miss having people care whether I was leaving
the house with a warm-enough jacket or what time I'd be home. Now,
I was accountable only to myself.

It didn't feel real until I closed the door behind them. I hung some clothes in my new wardrobe, made my bed and piled my bedside tables with magazines and photo frames. I knew I should feel elated, but it felt too weird. I was alone in a suburb I'd visited only a handful of times. I didn't have heating, so I dragged a portable heater between rooms as I unpacked. On the way to the supermarket to buy groceries for the first time, I passed a neighbour. 'Hi, I'm Nicole,' I smiled. She nodded and closed her apartment door behind her without uttering a word. Right, then.

After wandering up and down the supermarket aisles, choosing essentials carefully so they wouldn't blow the budget, I drove home. It was dark and I couldn't remember which backstreets I'd taken to arrive at Woolworths. I had to pull over, open Google Maps and work out where the hell I lived. When I got home, I stacked my groceries in my new fridge, an appliance purchased with a tiny space I'd freed up on my credit card before moving. I turned on the heater and the living room light. It flickered and warmed slowly before coming to life. I suspected the bulb would need replacing soon. I didn't have a step ladder. I wondered if my $35 Ikea coffee table (credit, again) would support my weight when I changed it.

I turned on the small TV that was also bought on credit and wrapped a blanket around myself while I waited for the heater to kick in. After lifting my favourite tea cup from a dusty box, I placed it on my second-hand dining table, took a picture and posted it on Instagram, with the caption 'First day of my new life'. Not pictured: me feeling overwhelmed. The sacrifices I'd made to save had felt hard enough, and now this was my reality for at least a year, maybe longer. I didn't feel at home. Not yet.

People often tell me how lucky I am to have an investment property, and I know I am. But in those first few weeks, 'lucky' is not the word I would have used. I was determined and I'd needed more than luck. You can afford to get into the property market if you reset your lifestyle expectations and save hard. But money is only part of the battle. I wish I'd known how much mental and emotional resilience would be required. I'm not telling you this to put you off. I'm telling you so you're more prepared than I was.

The way you prepare for such a challenge, of course, will depend on your situation. If you're renting with a partner, and later planning to buy together, you'll already be accustomed to your living arrangements. If you, like me, go from a family or a sharehouse to living on your own, it might be a good idea to set up a new routine that involves visiting people, playing sport or getting a hobby – anything that prevents you from suddenly, frequently being alone. Regardless of your circumstances, the one thing that will help you prepare is managing your expectations ... and your budget.

Here's the absolute minimum the first year cost me:

Monthly expenses

Having some sort of life: $600 ($150-ish per week)

Food and cleaning products: $350 ($70–80 per week)

Petrol: $200 (about $50 per week)

Mortgage repayments: $1550

Car repayments: $300

Credit cards: $350

Gas: $110

Electricity: $80

Private health insurance: $100

Car and home insurance: $70

Phone: $100

That's a total of about $3810 per month.

Each month, I was earning just over $4000 after tax at that point, so I should have had about $400 left over if I was really smart. But this figure doesn't allow for clothes, birthday presents, skincare or anything unexpected, like trips to the doctor or dentist. In the first year, I had some health problems and needed to see a specialist a few times. Do you think I'd budgeted for $200 specialist fees that weren't covered by my private health insurance policy? Nope. Then there was the occasional incidental: a parking fine, a broken appliance, small things that needed fixing around my home. You don't see those little expenses coming.

Plus, anything leftover at the end of the month had to be saved so I could afford my quarterly and yearly expenses. I was trying to save to install a split system so I would have air-conditioning by summer (spoiler: that didn't happen).

Quarterly expenses

Owners corporation fees: $350

Water: $200

Total: $550

My owners corporation fees were pretty reasonable in the first year – we put them up later when we discovered the property needed work. For now, thankfully, I could afford a quarterly $350 fee – only just, though. If I received a water bill and an owners corporation notice in the same month, my expenses were more than my income. During those months I'd shuffle payments around, putting little bits and pieces on my credit cards so I could struggle through.

The problem with my monthly and quarterly expenses being roughly the same as my income is that there was literally nothing left over for my annual expenses. So when my first council rates bill arrived, I did what anyone in my financial position would do: I ignored it.

The great thing about rates is they give you a heads up well in advance and there's an option to pay quarterly. Naturally, I didn't do that. Instead, I quietly panicked. Ditto with my car rego.

Annual expenses

Rates: $1100

Car registration: $800

Annual mortgage administration fee: $400

Total: $2300

Why the first year is the toughest

I thought money would be my biggest worry, but that was just one of the many woes I endured in the first year. I'd never lived alone before. More than anything, I struggled with the isolation. Coming home at the end of a stressful day only to be greeted by heavy silence took a long time to get used to. At first, I mentally reminded myself that I was finally paying off my own mortgage instead of someone else's. I was my own landlord and I could do whatever I wanted, whenever I wanted: leave dishes in the sink, throw a party, paint a feature wall, get a puppy.

This might have been more freeing if I'd had the money for a party, or cans of paint, or a puppy – but I didn't. So, from Monday to Friday, I'd do little more than get up in the dark to beat the traffic and drive more than an hour from Mordialloc to Richmond, work all day, drive home, make dinner, make my lunch for the next day and whiz up the smoothie I'd drink in the car on the following morning's commute, then fall into bed. I had to be in the car by 7.20 am to make it to the office by 9. Any later and I'd be crawling up the Nepean Highway, likely to arrive late. At the end of the day, I'd often stay late at work to avoid sitting in peak-hour traffic. Sometimes I took the train instead, but walking to the station, squeezing into a packed train and walking to the office took just as long.

I tried to give myself pep talks. *One year. You just have to get through one year*, I'd tell myself. Sometimes it worked, sometimes it didn't. My mind messed with me. I often imagined my inner-city friends out for drinks on a Thursday night, loving life, flirting with boys, eating tacos and burying their faces in oversized happy-hour margaritas while I chopped carrots and onions and listened to a newsreader deliver the day's headlines.

The self-induced emotional stress weighed far more than the stack of bills on my kitchen bench. I hadn't expected to feel like this. I thought being a homeowner would be like having a superpower. With the exception of the times I stayed at work drinking free booze, my most exhilarating Friday night during those first few months was one in which I treated myself to a cheap bottle of wine on the way home, ran a bath, put on an '80s playlist and sipped myself silly.

Mortgage broker Ben Ong says, 'You spend so much time putting the goal on the pedestal. It's not always what people expect.' That's because people often see the home itself, or the money to be made, not the impact on their day-to-day life. Whether you've looking for a home to live in or an investment, it's not just the physical cost and material fact of the property, it's how it fits into your life practice. 'It's the sum of the parts. You can't change the commute,' Ben says.

Nailed it, Ben. That commute and the sum of the parts definitely tested my sanity.

And another blow: it took a further toll on my personal life. I'd met a guy through friends and after a few dates I invited him around for dinner. I was excited to show him my apartment. He arrived and at first the banter was easy, but as I began to tell him about the process of buying he fell quiet. He'd just spent a fortune travelling the world, and was now crashing with a friend. He had almost nothing to his name.

'What would I bring to this?' He asked, which surprised me. 'Affection, emotional support,' I joked. But I could see something decisive tick over in his eyes. I wondered if he didn't see us as equals because I was ahead of him financially. His response reminded me of the way I'd behaved with prospective partners when I wasn't financially ready to make a commitment. I think previous generations were less concerned about settling down before they had set themselves up – they felt confident they'd be able to make a material life come together. But in my experience, today's extraordinary cost of living has many young people delaying relationships until they feel established, both professionally and financially.

Generation X and millennial women are the first to buy homes on their own in large numbers. This is the first time in history that we're testing that dynamic out on relationships. As a kid I read books and watched films and TV shows in which fairytale happy endings were the norm. I'd always assumed I'd buy a place with a partner, but now that I'd bought one on my own I was no longer a damsel in distress. I had rescued myself. I began to seriously consider what this meant for my future romances. The reality is that the complex business of money can become a serious issue in even the strongest relationship. If one party comes to the partnership with strong financial skills and perhaps some assets, while the other doesn't, it's something you need to negotiate as the relationship evolves.

The brief pleasure of having a guy around only served to highlight how nice it would be to have more company. I resolved to start doing two things after that: meet locals and start exercising again.

The latter was easier than the former. I've never been much of a swimmer, but on freezing nights, the local pool and its miraculously affordable casual swim prices provided warmth, a cheap reason not to go straight home and the endorphins I needed to press on. Soon enough it was spring and on a sunny Saturday I went to the beach and ran for kilometres. This part of the bay has white sand and azure waters to rival Queensland. It takes time to forge a meaningful connection with a new place, especially if you've never lived there before. With a bit of '90s pop in my earbuds, sun on my face and salty air messing my hair, I was beginning to love where I lived.

Around the same time, I downloaded a dating app and set the radius of options close to home. I flicked through the prospects and matched with Rob. When we met for a drink at a local bar, we discovered we'd both done the same thing: buying something small in an area we could afford in the hope of building on that humble investment over time. We had little else in common. He worked in some sort of corporate tech job in the city – I barely understood what he did. Sparks didn't exactly fly, but our shared life stage gave us enough of a reason to hang out from time to time. We were never going to be long-term partners, we both knew this, but he showed me local places to hang out and became my single strand of local community.

Meanwhile, I was dealing with another unique and previously undiscovered stress: owners corporation administration. I'd been warned about the associated owners corporation fees, which are a serious consideration for young homebuyers. Not only do you have your considerable mortgage to manage, but if you buy an apartment you'll be hit with quarterly owners corporation. costs, too. Mine were only a few hundred a quarter, but like anything you get what you pay for. At the time, I was one of two owner-occupiers in the block of six. I knew when I bought that there was some damage to the gutter at the front of the block that hadn't been repaired after a tree fell during a storm. There was a drain next to the carport that ran off into nothing – creating an epic puddle every time it rained. The hedge along the driveway needed a serious prune and the clothesline was unusably rusty, which I wouldn't have cared so much about if I had a dryer, but I didn't (that was part of the long-term wishlist). When I washed my sheets, I hung them from my bedroom doors to dry.

Naively, I emailed the owners corporation manager and asked for the hedge to be trimmed; and could we please get a new clothesline? He told me he'd get a couple of quotes. Months passed before I could get the estimates out of him. Then, when we'd agreed on one, he did nothing. The hedge continued to grow wildly out of control.

Just following up on your confirmation that the hedge would be trimmed last week, weather permitting. We've had no shortage of fine days for this to be completed and it hasn't been done yet. Please confirm when I can expect the hedge to be chopped right back to its original state. Currently I can barely get my car up the driveway when there's another car parked on the side.

That was just one of many emails. It took another two and a half weeks to get the hedge sorted. The clothesline took significantly longer. These weren't huge maintenance things. In the end, I called the guy and asked: 'Do you have a clothesline at your house?'

'Yes,' I recall him saying, sheepishly.

'Well, imagine what it's like living without one,' I replied.

I had a new clothesline the following week.

I'm aware that living without a clothesline is a first-world problem, but there was money in the dwindling fund to cover the cost of replacing the rusty one. We pay administration fees to have these things done. If you purchase an apartment, there are so many things that are out of your control. It's almost like renting and suffering the whims of a lazy landlord. *Almost.*

Given many of us will invest in apartments as a way to enter the market, I've learned it's essential to know as much about the owners corporation and its accounting process as possible. Join the committee. Make sure the property isn't in danger of falling into disrepair, and make your owners corporation fees work for you. If the manager isn't doing their job, pull them up on it.

Reducing costs with a tenant

About six months in, in late 2014, I listed my second bedroom on a sharehousing website in the hope that a flatmate would relieve some of the financial pressure and the isolation. I'd worked out that I could probably get $120 per week for the room, so if I was prepared to sacrifice space and privacy, I'd actually be able to afford to live a little.

But the market for sharehousing in Mordialloc isn't like it is in desirable suburbs closer to the city. At that time, the area mostly consisted of owner-occupiers, and while there was something of a rental market, there was a far lower demand for sharing. Airbnb could have been an option, but again, being so far out of town meant fewer applicants. Just two people responded to my listing. A divorced guy in his late thirties said it would be ideal for him, but was there enough room for a double bed and a small single? His child would be staying every second weekend. I wasn't against this in theory, but the room really wasn't big enough to accommodate one and a half people.

A young woman wielding a measuring tape arrived one Saturday morning to inspect the place and wasted no time pacing ahead of me to poke around. Getting on her hands and knees to size up the living room, she wondered aloud if her bookshelves would fit along the wall next to mine. 'Could you put them in the bedroom?' I asked. 'Maybe ...' she replied, 'If I could leave my bike in the lounge.'

I contemplated it. Having a bike leaning against the far wall wasn't a big deal. But then she asked if she could pay the bond about a month after moving in, and whether I was flexible with rental payments, because, well, being a student with a casual job her income was inconsistent. I said that I was afraid I would prefer the first month's rent and bond upfront. I closed the door knowing that my living room would remain configured just as it was. I decided sharing this place wasn't going to work. I'd look for other ways to make more cash.

Avos of wisdom

 The first year of home ownership can take some adjustment, both financially and mentally. Think about how life will change once your property has settled or you've moved in, and manage your expectations.

 Money issues can create friction in new and existing relationships. If you're in a partnership, aim to talk regularly and openly about your individual finances and how they might affect your relationship.

 If you're planning to be an owner-occupier and want to rent one of your rooms, look at the market for sharehousing or short-term rentals in the areas you are canvassing to see what the demand is like.

11

Surviving the Side Hustle

WITH RATES PAYMENTS AND OWNERS corporation fees both overdue and no bearable candidates to share my home, I began to wonder how long a human could feasibly live on canned tuna alone. I continued making minimum payments on each credit card, and forked out for basic groceries and petrol with the funds I'd temporarily freed up. Shelling out for water, electricity, gas, phone, car repayments, those bloody credit cards and general living expenses meant my social life was non-existent, and I could barely breathe. Good times.

It was now February 2015. I had absolutely no idea where I was going to find an extra $1100. I considered getting a weekend job in a bar. At least that way I might make a few local mates.

My friend Beck, who was working as a journalist at *The Australian Financial Review*, told me the editor was looking for someone to write the executive property column in the paper's 'Life and Leisure' section. 'Agents will send multimillion-dollar listings, you'll write a short blurb for each and place the copy and the images in Google Drive. Easy,' she told me. Shortly after that I was introduced to the editor. We emailed back and forth, and I started a few weeks later.

After work each night I'd come home and open my laptop. It was a work computer I carted to and from the office – my old freelance machine had carked it, and I obviously couldn't afford a separate one for personal use. The *AFR* editor had passed my details on to real estate agents and PR managers, so each day luxury listings dropped into my inbox. On the couch, in front of the TV, I'd sift through the best offerings around the country.

Country manors, restored 1850s mansions, beachfront villas, entire-floor penthouses and estates with nine-hole golf courses were all up for grabs. I'd shortlist a mix of elite properties in different states. That was simple. But it was a bit of a gossip column in so far as I had to name the vendor, their occupation and ideally their reason for selling. I quickly learned that vendors at the top end of the market are notoriously private: some would rather avoid being featured than being named, despite the excellent exposure. If their reason for selling was less than ideal – say, a divorce or a financial issue – they'd almost certainly decline.

This made my job harder. I'd fire off a stack of emails each evening, requesting these details, and I'd inevitably get responses the next day, so I'd furtively shoot back replies at lunchtime or on my phone between meetings, ensuring I'd gathered all the information I needed to write up the listing before my deadline. The extra work was tiring, but I loved seeing the new listings appear and learning about the market, even if it seemed like a foreign country compared to the property realm I was occupying. It had a strange way of motivating me. I'd look at beautifully restored beach shacks and think: one day, maybe one day.

By the middle of March, I'd made enough to pay my council rates (late ... but in full). This side hustle and its particular demands was a bit risky. I didn't want to jeopardise my actual job. I told my bosses that I was doing some freelance writing on the side, but I promised it wouldn't compromise the quality of my work. I never let that happen, but I did have a couple of close calls. I remember taking a call from my editor at the *AFR* one day while on a video shoot for The Royals. More space had become available in my pages and they'd need another five listings within twenty-four hours. I couldn't chase them up while I was on the clock, at the shoot, so I called a stack of contacts after work and managed to gather together the intel I needed. I stayed up late writing them and then rose at 5 am to do the rest before work the next day.

I made my deadline, just. But I was stressed out of my mind. I'd replaced the anxiety of not paying bills on time with the pressure of a second job. But there was no way I was giving up this gig. It would help me get ahead.

So, you can imagine my delight in June 2015 when then treasurer Joe Hockey casually suggested that people who aspired to home ownership should simply 'get a good job that pays good money'. I was stunned. Nope, Joe, NOPE.

I had a 'good job'. I also had a university degree and a HECS debt that I was still chipping away at. Despite a decade of professional work experience and a good job, my little apartment and all the expenses that came with it were bleeding me dry. Clearly, a 'good' job wasn't enough. A *great* job that pays *exceptionally* might work. Being one half of a successful dual-income household would also be beneficial. But for the rest of us, there's a side hustle. That's right, Joe. *Two jobs*.

Writing the listings was eye-opening because sometimes I'd learn how the seller had made their fortune. Often, they'd simply bought well before the boom and sat on their property for decades while prices rose. In other cases, they were extremely successful businesspeople.

Here's a listing from 2015:

[Names Redacted], owners of [Property Company], are selling their country residence, which had its origins in 1873. The property, set on a

hectare, has eight bedrooms, five bathrooms, high ceilings, large living and dining rooms, a media room and outdoor entertaining areas. It also has parking for six cars, a wine cellar, established gardens and a barn.

Parking for six cars? It's on a bloody hectare. You could hold a ute muster in the front yard. I figured they were the kind of people old mate Hockey was talking about when he said it was easy to achieve home ownership. There's having a good job and then there's having a freaking empire.

Some weeks my editor would request five listings, sometimes ten. Occasionally ten listings and a 'suburb profile', a short piece profiling an area, its median price, recent growth stats and the pros and cons of buying in the 'hood. I said yes to every request. I'd already done my first year in Mordialloc and I wasn't even close to solvent enough to move back into a rental closer to the city. But if I could get my finances in order, maybe, in six months or so, I could.

I could make an extra two or three thousand each month on top of my salary – which would have been great, but I was now making so much that the tax office started hitting me up for regular pay as you go (PAYG) tax bills, so half of what I made went straight back to Joe and his mates in Canberra. Still, the extra cash made a difference, gradually. For the first time since I'd moved into my own home I was paying my bills comfortably and on time. Having a second job is not ideal. I'm not sure I could have done it if I had to look after anyone else. If you have a family and you're hustling, I tip my hat. You are extraordinary.

What you need to know about a second income

You mightn't be asked to pay tax before your return is due, but you'll need to declare the income when you do a tax return and you'll be taxed accordingly, so it's best to be prepared. Put half of what you make aside and don't touch it. In the event that your side gig brings in more than $75,000 a year, you'll also need to register for GST via the

ATO. It depends on what your second job is, but in my case I needed an ABN so I could invoice for my work. I put 50 per cent of everything I earned in a separate account so that I was covered when the tax bills hit. Importantly, be honest with your employer. You'll need to make sure there's nothing in your contract about taking on additional work, particularly if there's potential for a conflict of interest, or working for a competitor.

A personal motivation can help you keep up the stamina. Choosing a side hustle that helps you advance your career, either by gathering more skills, or by expanding your network or portfolio, could be a good incentive. For example, you might offer to manage the social media for a small business if you'd like to add that skill to your CV. If you're already working full-time, like I was, getting some pleasure out of the side hustle is crucial. I couldn't have worked all day and then gone home and done more hours if I didn't enjoy the work. It would have broken me.

A side hustle needs an end point

I'm not the only one who has hustled in the first year of managing a mortgage. In many cases, taking on additional work not only helps to make ends meet, it builds a financial buffer for cases of emergency. It's still a massive undertaking. Working two jobs robs people of leisure time, sleep and the opportunity to recharge. I'm a side-hustle advocate, but with this disclaimer: it's not sustainable long-term. At some point, being sleep-deprived and leading an unbalanced life is going to have a physical and emotional impact. I found this out the hard way.

Taking on a second job in the first year of home ownership would always have a foreseeable end date for Bec Killen. In June 2018, Bec and her husband, Dan, bought their home in Queensland's Caboolture South, about 45 kilometres north of Brisbane. The area has a mix of older weatherboard Queenslanderers and new estates. Bec and Dan bought in an estate that they like because it's family-friendly and quiet. They settled on the location because it's close to Dan's son and not too far from the beach.

After saving a 20 per cent deposit over two years, they secured their brand-new three-bedroom, two-bathroom home, with a front garden, a decent backyard and solar panels, for $387,500. 'We worked our butts off and sacrificed luxuries,' Bec says, recalling the period of saving for the deposit. But that was just the beginning. Bec, thirty-four, worked two jobs: in disability and mental health community services. In her primary role, she juggles numerous responsibilities, including administration and suicide prevention support work. In her second position, she supported a woman with a severe brain injury, working with her on weekends, taking sleepover or 24-hour shifts to ensure her client had everything she needed at all times. Between the two roles, she worked sixty to seventy hours per week. Dan works as a geologist. As far as side hustles go, Bec's was tough. 'I'd go straight from my main job to my second job and assist her in all facets of her life,' she explains.

'I'm also studying full-time online, so our social lives suffer a bit,' she says. Bec steals any moment possible to keep up with the work required for her Diploma of Mental Health. 'I study in my lunchbreaks and at night. Sometimes I study when I'm travelling to and from work on the train.'

The aim was to save enough to feel comfortable. Knowing what they know now, Bec and Dan would have made sure they had more up their sleeve for anything that went wrong, even ostensibly small things like connection fees – these all add to the monumental costs of the first year.

Unsurprisingly, having two physically and emotionally demanding jobs made Bec absolutely exhausted. In November 2018, she completed her last disability support shift, knowing that the way she was operating couldn't have continued forever, as nice as the extra cash was. 'I am quite happy with the amount of back-up funds we have,' she says and adds, 'We are going to keep the money mainly for emergencies.'

The sacrifice is definitely worth it. 'We are no longer renters, we can do what we want with the house and it makes us feel secure to have a place of our own, rather than paying off someone else's mortgage,' Bec says. Now that they're comfortable with their little pot of reserve funds, Bec has returned to enjoying her life. 'I'm able to dedicate more time to my family and also able to do a lot more study and get my diploma finished quicker,' she explains. 'I'm home of a night and weekend, which I think is really important for family time.'

Budgeting for the first year of home ownership

Saving for a house deposit should help to get you into good habits for the first year of ownership, but I also encourage you to be in a better financial position than I was when I finally bought my apartment. At the very least, you want to still have some funds up your sleeve once you've settled the property. In fact, you'll have to be financially fitter than I was. According to financial adviser Ryan Watson, banks are now going through your transaction history 'line by line' over a three- to six-month period. They're looking at everything from the frequency of UberEats deliveries to gym memberships and other 'discretionary spending' habits that might work against you.

Since banks tightened their lending, people are increasingly aware that their transaction history has to be virtuous well before they apply for a loan. 'We have someone who's come to us two years out,' Ryan says. It's now that important to have a reliable transaction history that shows you're able to live well within your means before you get approved. For your own sanity it's smart to have a 'one-month savings buffer', and it's reassuring to have $3000 to $5000 on hand after you settle. It would have been nice to have an extra $5000 on hand in my first year. That would have covered my big bills.

'If you're taking on too much debt, you're going to be awake at night,' Ryan says. Ideally, when you start saving your deposit, it's better to have an idea of what you can afford to buy and what you can afford to service. My mistake was thinking that because I could afford the mortgage repayments, I'd be fine. I hadn't properly factored in owners corporation fees, rates, bills or living expenses. If you're clear about what you're up for after you sign on the dotted line and have an income that covers those costs, you shouldn't have to do it so tough. It might mean buying something cheaper than you'd ideally like, but overextending yourself for a home is really stressful. If you can avoid it, you don't want to question your decision, which is what I went on to do.

Avos of wisdom

 Consider creating a budget for the first year so you're aware of – and can prepare for – upcoming expenses at all times.

 Look at ways to generate additional income, such as renting a room out or taking on a second job – but remember, having a side hustle takes its toll.

 Try to build a 'savings buffer' so you're able to cover unexpected costs.

12

Is It Worth It?

ON A SUNDAY AFTERNOON, I pulled into the driveway with a car full of groceries, opened the boot of my little hatchback, collected some bags and hauled them upstairs to my first-floor apartment. I came back down for more to find a dead bird on the back seat. In the time it had taken me to dump the bag in the kitchen and return, a bird had flown in through the boot, panicked and thrashed around, hitting the windows.

After recovering from the shock of discovering the poor grey-feathered sparrow lying there lifeless, I knocked on my ground-floor neighbour's door and explained what had happened. He kindly collected the bird with a dustpan and broom and removed it for me. I went upstairs, grabbed my vacuum cleaner, plugged it into his kitchen socket and sucked up the feathers that were scattered around my car.

This could happen to anyone of course – whether they own a home or not is immaterial – but, for whatever reason, this unsettling incident was the moment I began to wonder: *has this been worth it?*

Once I'd parked my car and put the vacuum away, I decided I was ready for something to change. I wouldn't rush into it, but it was time to start thinking about the process of turning my home into an investment. It was time to start working towards the pay-off, so that I could confidently say, *Yes. Yes, this has been worth it*. At that moment I really wasn't sure it had been.

A few weeks earlier, my smoke detector had started beeping in the middle of the night. The unexpected ear-splitting sound pierced my deep sleep and in moments had me bolt upright. I switched on my bedroom light, rubbed my eyes and realised the batteries probably needed replacing. Grabbing a chair from the living room, I wobbled precariously while trying to eject the batteries, but they were stuck. Tired and frustrated, I ripped the whole contraption out of the ceiling, collecting part of it in my hand and leaving exposed wires hanging. I stepped off the chair, dusted the white plaster flakes I was covered with out of my hair and off my shoulders, and returned to bed. I'd clean up in the morning.

This too was a turning point. I'd given up so much for the dream of home ownership. I wasn't seeing my friends as much as I might have if I lived closer to them. I wasn't taking holidays or travelling. I wasn't entertaining or dating or reading or volunteering – or doing anything much beyond work. I had two jobs. I was exhausted. And lonely. I'd grown accustomed to having my own space, but the commute and working around the clock were taking their toll. I felt alone in my pursuit; I longed to have someone in it with me.

I can understand why some of my millennial mates have accepted their fate as lifelong renters, saying 'screw it' to mortgages – travelling and shopping and dining out instead. It's bloody hard to save a deposit and find a property. Then, just when you think you've made it, you become the butt of a sick joke: managing the financial burden that comes with actually owning it. These are the best years of our lives.

I feared I was squandering mine.

And yet, there was a positive side effect that I hadn't anticipated. I was officially 'adulting'. Through the challenges that came with saving, managing a mortgage, dealing with an owners corporation and a temperamental smoke detector, I was growing a thicker skin. If I hadn't pulled my head in and dealt with my spending demons, I could have stayed suspended in an endless adolescence. Fun into my thirties … perhaps. But the rumbling anxiety about my financial future would be getting louder and louder, surely taking a mental toll. On the other hand, how would I feel now if I'd selected a different path? Sharehouses have their social benefits. I might have stayed in one and indulged in the luxury of being a full-time freelance writer. As I thought about how hard it is to get ahead without giving up at least some personal aspirations, I decided ultimately that my decisions would turn out to have been worth it. I wouldn't regret them, as long as I turned my efforts into positive results moving forward.

I'm not alone in moving further away from friends, family and work to get ahead. Matt Stonehouse grew up in Melbourne's inner-eastern suburbs, but he knew he'd never be able to afford a first home where he'd lived as a kid. 'We would have loved to stay in the city, but we bit the bullet,' he says. Matt and his wife, Ebony, worked hard to save a deposit. In 2009, they bought a home on a block of land in Frankston South, 43 kilometres from Melbourne's CBD. They spent $350,000, renovated and then sold in 2012 for $200,000 more than they paid.

For Matt, a thirty-seven-year-old qualified carpenter, moving further out has been worth it. He saw the potential in going out on his own and starting a business. He founded his residential building company in 2012, with friend Vincent Price. Initially they took on private refurbishments, but soon they had enough equity in the business to build their own developments. They've since completed two properties, one in Mount Martha and the other in Mornington, both on

Victoria's in-demand Mornington Peninsula. Matt believes the key to success in property is buying in outer suburbs that are supported by strong amenities and infrastructure – 'Whether it's schools, shopping centres or transport,' he says.

Home ownership won't be for everyone. I'm acutely aware that I was extremely fortunate to have parents who let me come home to save, and this sped the process up. If buying was completely off the cards, I would still have hustled and eventually invested in something. At some point, I felt I had to grow up, suffer through the shit bits that come with a significant sacrifice and hope that it would one day pay dividends. When I had to pull a smoke detector from the ceiling, it was comforting to know I had damaged *my* plaster, not someone else's.

Why property remains a good investment

In 2018, prices in some parts of the country dropped in a way we hadn't seen since the global financial crisis and everyone got in a tizz. Some media outlets were beating up the figures, predicting declines of up to 40 per cent.

Nerida Conisbee, realestate.com.au's chief economist, who I spoke to in late 2018 set the record straight, explaining that, yes, prices did indeed drop in Sydney and Melbourne, but it was far from a national crisis. 'Adelaide is at its highest median ever recorded; Hobart and Canberra had double-digit growth,' she clarifies. A number of factors influenced the falls, including the tightening of lending and more conservative investor behaviour, but this was mostly good news for millennial first home buyers. Revised first-homebuyer incentives enabled many young people to enter the market. In fact, we had the 'highest first-homebuyer finance approvals in almost a decade,' Nerida says.

'The big driver has been in New South Wales,' she explains. That was a result of the removal of stamp duty on homes worth up to

$650,000, and additional concessions on properties worth more. For Sydney-based aspiring homebuyers, falling prices and improved incentives provided a sense that ownership was actually achievable, and many successfully danced their way into these changing conditions.

Despite tighter lending, Nerida says that first home buyers didn't have too much trouble getting finance like investors did. 'First home buyers are typically in it for the long haul and they're buying at lower price points. Their incomes are going to increase, and in some cases they are dual income, which makes them lower risk than an investor.' By contrast, she says, 'An investor could get into trouble if they've taken on too much debt, or they might not have long-term income like younger buyers.'

So, if prices have stagnated, but there are incentives to enter the market, is property still a good long-term investment? Yes, it is. 'I'd always recommend people buy something,' Nerida says. But, she explains, that's not necessarily because purchasing property is a guarantee that you're going to pocket a stack of cash. 'In any market there are increases and declines – it isn't a done deal that housing will increase for the rest of our lives.' The main reason property is a good investment is actually because, she suggests, 'Most people aren't very good savers – it's a form of enforced saving – if you have a loan, you pay it back.' Plus, a primary home is a tax-free asset. Regardless of fluctuating markets and prices, you'll ultimately pay down an investment that you can live in, which becomes increasingly important as we age. 'Once you hit retirement you are in a vastly different situation if you own your own home than if you're still renting.' Currently in Australia, the age pension is calculated without including the family home as an asset. On the flipside, renting on a pension can leave you pretty vulnerable. 'If you're in an area where rents are rising rapidly, you're trapped in the market. If you own your home, you're not,' Nerrida warns.

And of course you don't have to wait for retirement – the benefits of property ownership kick in well before that. Nerida uses the inner-city suburb of Richmond in Melbourne as an example. If I'd bought in this suburb ten years ago, my loan repayments would have been about the same as renting. Now, I'd be paying a much higher portion of my income in rent and I'd have no asset to show for it. 'If you want to live there long-term, then buying typically does make more sense,' she explains.

While it's impossible to predict where prices will go, Nerida says, 'We probably won't see the same level of growth over the next decade as we have over the last decade, but we probably won't see massive falls.' With population growth remaining steady in Sydney and Melbourne, as well as in smaller cities, there is plenty to be optimistic about for those getting into the market in coming years. If you're looking to invest and live elsewhere, Nerida points to places such as Hobart. 'There has been strong growth over the past four to five years there. That's probably coming to an end, but there are nice homes at an affordable price and economic growth is still occurring.' Brisbane has reasonably priced apartments, she also notes, while in Adelaide 'the price points are very attractive for someone looking for a first investment'. But, she cautions, buying in a state you don't live in requires research. 'If it's not a market you understand, you need to be careful.' She draws on the difference between Adelaide, which is a growing city, and Coober Pedy, which is more than 800 kilometres north of Adelaide to point out some of the distinctions. Aside from the obvious difference between city and remote location, there is the dramatic variance in price. You can get a house in Coober Pedy for less than $100,000 and Nerida says there's an 'amazing rental yield' there, but there's also little to no capital growth, which means your property may not rise in value for years, if at all. So while it might cost more to enter the Adelaide market, it might make more sense from a capital growth perspective, if that's your objective.

Working out your trade-offs

I thought I'd made a lot of sacrifices to get into the property market. Then I met Nathan and Lucy Hersey. They've hustled harder than anyone I've met to achieve their property dreams and after meeting them at their home in the tiny village of Loch, I'm convinced that the key to success is a sustained commitment to sacrifice, which is achievable if those sacrifices are in line with your values and long-term goals.

The little retail strip at Loch, a town established in 1876 in Victoria's South Gippsland, has historic shops, a red brick brewery and the harvested provisions of a strong local farming community. Here they take fresh produce and good living seriously. The land is affordable and it's only a seventy-five minute drive from Melbourne's CBD. It took Lucy, twenty-seven, and Nathan, thirty, a while to get here, though.

Their property journey began back in 2011, after the pair started dating. While studying, Nathan worked three jobs: in a restaurant, a call centre and a nightclub. At twenty-four he had managed to save a deposit for a house. He set his sights on a rundown three-bedroom deceased estate in the Mornington Peninsula suburb of Rosebud. It was auctioned at 2 pm on Melbourne Cup Day and only a handful of people were in attendance. Lucy and Nathan were both working, so Nathan's mum went to bid on their behalf. She cheekily opened the bidding at $150,000, which Lucy says stalled the action. 'I guess the other parties worried she knew something about the house that they didn't.' In the end, they secured the home for just over $300,000. Nathan had two cousins renting the other rooms at first, but in 2012 they moved out and Lucy moved in.

Lucy and Nathan's first renovation project in 2013 involved fixing up a pale blue vintage caravan they named 'Franklin'. 'It was a mouldy shell rusting in a paddock and we turned it into a cute little travelling cafe,' Lucy recalls, 'It was our first go on the tools.' They ran the cafe while working full-time for three years, at which point their side hustle had earned them enough extra cash to sell the business and take on bigger property projects.

Prices in Rosebud had been rising fast. The area has always been a popular spot for holidaymakers, and inflated demand inspired existing owners sitting on large blocks to profit from subdividing. After cottoning on, Lucy and Nathan started the process themselves, and by 2016 they had a small parcel to sell.

With the profits from the subdivision, they were able to buy thirty-seven acres in South Gippsland. It'd been on the market for a while and had been neglected. 'I guess not many people get chuffed about elimination of noxious weeds, but that's what floats our boat – turning something nobody wants into something valuable again,' Lucy says. Here they tackled their first build: an off-the-grid shack made of recycled materials. The long-term plan for the property is to produce specialty goods, including pasture-raised beef and flowers. They've called it 'Sky Pastures Farm'.

Lucy works as a research assistant at Monash University in Clayton and Nathan is a political adviser in Frankston. For now, they're based in Rosebud and they commute to their jobs. How have they managed to pull all this off in a matter of years? The formula is actually really easy to get right: 'We live pretty simply and save a lot of our income,' Lucy says.

Their latest venture is a bigger one. In addition to the farm, the pair were looking for an investment in South Gippsland, and they set their sights on Loch. 'We missed out on a house after making a couple of offers and then saw the block and decided to build,' Lucy explains. But after running the numbers on a new build, they wondered if there was a smarter option. Property developers and people replacing old homes with new ones often discard perfectly good properties so they can build their shiny new developments. Depressing as that is, it means period homes are up for grabs – and they go for next to nothing as long as you're prepared to pay for the relocation. 'Nathan had always loved the idea of rescuing a heritage house, so the plan to move something destined for demolition was born.' Their 107-year-old home 'The Windsor Loch' was saved and transported from Mont Albert in Melbourne's inner east on a truck a few months after they bought the block in September 2017.

But if you reckon this is a great idea, Lucy warns that you're better off having a chunk of the funds ready. 'It was actually really difficult to get a loan for a house relocation, because it's not an existing house, it's not a new build and so it has no value according to the bank,' she says. Fortunately, they'd paid down a fair bit of the Rosebud mortgage and owned the farm outright; they had equity to borrow against, which improved their position slightly.

Lucy and Nathan found their dream shack through a company called Moving Views. Scroll through the list of available homes on the website and you'll find dwellings in varying conditions available for $100,000 to $200,000. Although it's a long process, it's easy to see why purchasing a historic home and moving it to an affordable piece of land is appealing.

The couple shuffled their savings and a couple of personal loans to fund the relocation. Once the building had arrived at Loch, they could refinance and consolidate the project as one loan. This was their riskiest undertaking yet and a massive stretch financially, but, Lucy says, 'You have to take risks, I think. We are still young and don't have babies to provide for so it's perfectly fine to live on toasted sandwiches for a while at this stage.'

Thanks to their resourcefulness, the beautiful four-bedroom Edwardian home, which had an extension added in the 1970s, avoided a regrettable end. Built in 1912, it has magnificent high ceilings, original floors, large front windows with shutters and leadlight details.

The house was far from perfect when it was offloaded from the truck in three parts, though. Trailing behind it on the South Gippsland Highway as it was being moved in February 2018, Lucy and Nathan watched as part of their hallway wall fell onto the bitumen and exploded in a puff of plaster smoke. 'Oh, there's part of our house,' Lucy said to Nathan as they drove past the debris. They weren't worried, though. Part of the contract required Moving Views to replaster walls damaged in relocation. It took months for the team to piece the house back together and there were delays. Nathan also later found out that other clients had pushed harder for completion, so the duo's polite patience meant their property sat on the backburner.

We're standing in the living room ten months after the house arrived and there's still heaps to do, but it's coming together. On the day I visit, they're both in their workwear and a tradie mate is in the yard giving them a hand. There's a picnic basket full of food on the bench, and a mattress in the front room where they can take alternating breaks. Seeing the completed structure finally on the land and reassembled should have been rewarding, but when she walked in for the first time Lucy burst into tears. 'I thought, "What have we done? We've spent all of or savings on this and it's just a shell. There's rain coming in. We've made a terrible mistake".' In recent months they've added new ceiling roses and renovated the kitchen themselves. Nathan taught himself to make a benchtop and doing all the work on their own has meant that that room, with new appliances and repainted cupboards, came together for less than $3000. Now, they're painting, fixing the floors and tending to the minor details so the house will soon be ready for furniture. The place is coming together.

'A lot of people don't want to spend their weekend doing this,' Nathan says. 'If your motivation is to go out and socialise and get pissed all the time that's what you're spending your money on. Some people have criticised us, they've said you work too much. But we enjoy this.' He recalls living in a rental before he bought. The owner had paid $7500 for the block and $7500 for the home in 1975. 'We shouldn't be paying what we pay now for houses. It's ridiculous – out of control.' Like most millennials, Nathan and Lucy can see the inequality a new generation of homebuyers face. But his philosophy is: you can get down about it, or you can get on with it. He's quick to add that 'It's not always rose-coloured glasses' when it comes to the good old days of cheaper property. His parents had their own worries at his age. 'They talk about when interest rates were high. My dad got locked out of his job because of an industrial dispute. The economy was struggling.'

As they've sourced materials for the house, Nathan says they've been struck by people's kind feedback. 'People think there's a mentality that young people want everything now and they don't want to work for it. I got this handrail at the front from a guy, he said, "I'm just so happy to see young people having a go." It was really nice.'

Even with the reno factored in, the land, house, relocation and refurb will have cost them about $340,000 all up. Not too shabby, but what makes it affordable is the fact that they're attempting the whole makeover on their own, engaging specialists only for the technical stuff like plumbing and rewiring. 'We have learned how to use the power tools and made plenty of mistakes so far. I'm sure we will stumble our way through. We have tradie friends we can turn to for advice,' Lucy says. They plan to have a rest when their home is completed. Working around the clock isn't sustainable – they know that. But they understood that they would have to struggle to get ahead. 'We figure working hard while we're young will pay off later,' Lucy says.

There's little doubt that sitting on their front deck with a cuppa will make it all worthwhile. They look forward to being able to reflect on their journey and say: 'We did it ourselves.' It'll be a satisfying moment. Nathan jokes that it's their million-dollar home, because when it was in Mont Albert it sold for $1.4 million. Driving away, I have to agree: a million-dollar home is where the heart is.

Avos of Wisdom

 Be prepared to take a step back to move forward. You might have to move further out than you'd like, but it doesn't have to be forever.

 Mortgage repayments might seem daunting, but like Nerida says, 'It's a form of enforced saving – if you have a loan, you pay it back.' At the end of that loan, you have an asset.

 Lucy and Nathan's story shows that working hard pays off. They're smart getting it done while they're young.

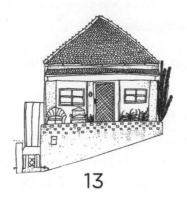

13

Reaping the Benefits

TWELVE MONTHS IN MORDIALLOC HAD come and gone. To celebrate, I threw a housewarming in June 2015. I hadn't done it earlier because I didn't even have enough spare cash for cheese platters and I was hardly going to hold a party in an unheated apartment in the middle of winter. But now, thanks to my side hustle, I'd saved enough for a split-system. Besides, I'd spent a year traipsing to see my inner-city friends, and some hadn't even seen my home yet. (I probably would have been more disappointed about this if they hadn't provided me with couches to sleep on.) I was genuinely quite surprised to find that after I posted the Facebook invitation almost every person on the list made the effort.

When some of my work friends moaned about the distance they'd be travelling, I rolled my eyes. 'Try doing it *every day*.' One couple rocked up and greeted me with their review of the Frankston trainline: a riot, 'an hour of entertainment for the cost of a fare'. People could poke fun at my chosen suburb as much as they liked. Everything was starting to click into place now – I could see the light. It didn't feel quite so hard anymore and I was proud that I'd pulled off a year of home ownership on my own.

Working with an owners corporation

There was just one more thing that I had to deal with: my bloody owners corporation management.

Over the course of the year, I'd gathered the contact details of the other owners. To do this, I had to request their email addresses and phone numbers via my useless manager. I told them about the challenges I'd faced getting things done and explained that there was more work required. The property looked like shit, quite frankly. The hedge wasn't getting trimmed as frequently as it should, the back fence was falling down and the gutters needed love. We had to spend a bit more so it wasn't the worst block in a lovely street.

Each year, there's an annual general meeting, to which all the owners are invited in order to assess the previous year's minutes and put new business on the agenda. I hadn't attended in 2014, as I'd just moved in and had work commitments. At that time I didn't understand how important it was.

By September 2015, I had more than a year of experience dealing with a second-rate manager, whose poor performance was potentially impacting the value of my property. Of the six owners, I was the only one who planned to attend the meeting. As the sole attendee, I set the location: my living room. I'd spoken to this guy and emailed him plenty of times, but when I saw him in person I realised exactly what the problem was. He was in his fifties, wearing an ill-fitting pair of suit pants and an old, thinning cotton shirt. He carried a briefcase (um, okay ...) and from it he produced a number of cardboard folders and a scattering of receipts and maintenance quotes. It was no wonder our administrative affairs were a mess – our manager was operating like it was 1979.

I'd collected proxy votes from other investors and at the end of the meeting I elected to have the owners corporation removed and replaced. Closing the door behind him, I felt a little stunned. How did I land in a position where I was calling the shots for the whole building? It was pretty simple, actually: I cared the most. I was one of two owner-occupiers and the other owner-occupier was preparing to sell. While one investor was interested, the other three weren't particularly fussed. But for me, this was my actual home and my only investment. I'd never intended to buy in a large block and I was grateful that I'd only had to wrangle five other people to get things done.

After the AGM, I contacted all the owners to let them know the manager had been replaced. In the lead up to giving him the sack, I'd sourced an alternative. 'The immediate issues being investigated include plumbing concerns impacting the structure of the property and responding to issues raised in an engineer's report prepared in 2012 that have still not been addressed,' I explained. 'The intention is to prioritise the works required over time to bring the property back to life, hopefully without adjusting the quarterly levies.' If you'd told me a few years prior that I'd be sending emails like that, man, I would have laughed and ordered another wine. But it felt good to be learning about the building management. It didn't take long to work out that we needed to increase the levies from $350 to $750 per quarter to fund some of the larger jobs. It was a lot for a building without a lift or any other slick features. I certainly didn't want to spend that much more, but either we got the extra funds in the pot now to improve the block or we'd face serious costs later.

And ... breathe out

My initial plan to suck up my advertising agency job for a year was thrown out the window when I realised how much I loved the place. Despite overindulging in every perk that was thrown my way, I'd managed to take a few steps up the ladder and was now working on big branded content projects for major clients. With a pay rise and regular money coming in from the second job, I'd built up a buffer that was helping me prepare to make the move from Mordialloc to my ideal rental suburb: Richmond, not far from Melbourne's CBD. If I pulled it off, I'd be living moments from the office – commuting would be cancelled.

But there was something more pressing on the agenda: travel. I had the opportunity to hit South by Southwest, a music and media festival in Austin, Texas, early in 2016 with some of my work crew. The Royals would pay for my festival pass and accommodation if I could cover flights and spending money. Hell, yes, I could. I started budgeting for that, too. I'd actually managed to pay down a bit of the debt on one of my credit card, making room for flights. I booked for Texas, and after that I stopped trying to pay off the cards and just focused on putting away enough money to move after I returned from the US. Rough calculations showed I'd be in a position to move to Richmond around April 2016, as long as I kept doing the *Australian Financial Review* work on the side. In the meantime, I'd unfurrow my brow and lighten up.

Positive versus negative gearing

Once I moved, my property would be available for lease. Before I made this transition from owner-occupier to rentvestor, I began learning about its financial implications. I looked at similar two-bedroom units on real estate websites to get an idea of what sort of weekly rental they were attracting. I estimated that I might be able to get about $1200 per month. I would need to find the extra $300 each month to cover the rest of the mortgage.

This meant my property would be negatively geared. The advantage of negative gearing is that you can claim the interest component of the loan repayments and some of the other costs as an expense at tax time. You don't get the money back as such; it's offset against your income and can potentially improve your tax return instead.

Negative gearing is controversial. Not only has it been a way for people to keep their taxable income down, but many argue that it's a benefit for people who are already successfully building wealth. Not only do they have enough money to purchase an investment property, they enjoy rental income and a very likely growth in property value over time. It's polarising for those reasons. In particular, members of the boomer generation with already significant property portfolios benefit from negative gearing. An end to negative gearing was floated at the last federal election, but as it stands the financial structure remains in place. Here's how it works.

When it comes time to lodge your tax return, you give your accountant all the statements and bills related to costs incurred on your investment property during that financial year. These include things like:

Interest paid on the mortgage repayments

Property management fees

Maintenance you've paid for

Council rates

Water bills

Property insurance

Your total out-of-pocket expenses are deducted from your taxable income, and ideally your tax return will offset the amount your property has cost you.

It's important, however, that you have the money to cover those costs at the time, because you don't get your return until after the financial year has finished. For me, this involved being able to cover the mortgage gap, property management by the local agent, rates, water and insurance, as well as my own rent, wherever I moved to. I had hoped to be able to get a nice one-bedroom apartment in Richmond, but I couldn't afford to spend any more than I already was. That meant my budget was $1200 per month for rental, so I could still afford the extra $300 a month for Mordialloc that wouldn't be covered by my tenant's rent.

If your mortgage is $1000 per month and you have a tenant paying $1500, this might cover your mortgage and additional out-of-pocket expenses, in which case you're *positively geared*. Your tenant is covering the whole amount and you're pocketing an extra $500 per month, so you don't receive any benefits at tax time, and in fact you have to pay tax on that extra income.

Becoming a rentvestor

By December 2015, I'd done eighteen months in the apartment – longer than I'd planned, but thanks to my side gig with the *AFR* I could finally afford to seriously think about moving. By the time I started looking at rental options, I found the cost of a one-bedroom place was about the same as my mortgage. I was ideally looking for something cheaper, and that meant potentially returning to sharehousing.

I wasn't in a rush to start the transition. I worried about the leap of faith required. Should I find a Richmond property and then put my apartment up for rent? Or should I secure the tenant for Mordialloc first and then make the move? Either way, I had to find the cash to cover my first month's rent and bond in the new place, plus moving costs, and hopefully have enough left to cover my mortgage if I couldn't find a tenant right away. By my calculations, I needed about $5500 to do it. It'd be tight, but I could stretch the budget. Just.

In March 2016, my workmate Dom told me he was moving out of his humble two-bedroom Richmond worker's cottage and asked if I wanted to check it out. He took me to see it one night after work. My first thought: it's unbearably hot in here. 'No air-con,' Dom said, reading my mind. Sure, there were some cracks in the walls and the oven was pretty old, but I could hold a dinner party for forty in the massive main bedroom. The pressed-metal ceilings were magnificent and there was a timber deck to the side of the living room that was crying out for fairy lights and a few chairs. The best bit? It was cheap. About $1700 per month. With a tenant in the second room, my living costs were going to drop from $1500 per month to between $800 and $900. Even with the $300 mortgage gap, I was looking at $1200 total. I couldn't believe my luck. I could tolerate a few hot nights.

It was a private rental, so Dom passed the landlord's mobile number to me and we had a chat. I explained that I'd be moving out of my property and needed to find a tenant. Ideally I wanted three weeks to a month, but I didn't want to miss the opportunity to secure the place so I'd move as soon as he needed. Thankfully, he was an easygoing bloke. 'Start getting sorted and keep me posted,' he said.

I called a local agent the next day. A property manager came to assess my apartment, then a photographer took pictures and it was listed on real estate websites about forty-eight hours later. The property manager was confident I'd find someone quickly, so I locked in Richmond for after my trip to Texas. I couldn't wait to kick back on that deck with a glass of wine.

But I wouldn't forget about Mordialloc. In the interim, another owner-occupier had moved into the block and we'd bonded over our shared interest in making sure our investment was in good shape. As an accountant he could interrogate the numbers the owners corporation manager presented us with and make sure our quarterly payments were working for us. He joined the committee along with another owner, and we prepared a scope of work to continue improving the site in stages. To keep things moving we sourced our own quotes for repairs and reviewed unnecessary spending. We'd been paying a company to put the bins out on the street each week, so we cancelled it. The caretaker was paid too much for too little, so they were replaced with a more affordable company. A long-term plan was put in place to improve the building's facade. Without a shared vision, these things were unlikely to have unfolded.

Things to consider as a landlord

It was unsettling to imagine a stranger was going to move into a property I'd worked so hard to call my own. Despite knowing I'd lease it one day, I hadn't looked seriously at the demand for rentals in the area after I purchased. Since that time in 2014, a few new developments had sprung up in the area. A strengthening market is great, but it also means a steady supply of new properties. If there is an oversupply and there aren't enough renters to populate the available options, you run the risk of struggling to find a quality tenant. I worried that all the prospective tenants would be going for the brand-new properties instead of my place. What would happen if I couldn't find the right person?

Vacancy rates differ from suburb to suburb. In some places, there are more owner-occupiers and less of a demand for rentals. When my property was listed, vacancy rates were low in Mordialloc, but, on the flipside, the suburb had a healthy number of owner-occupiers. My agent was confident I'd find a good tenant. She was really empathetic about my fears of finding a good applicant without it sitting empty for too long. If a property is vacant for a while, it's probably because the landlord's asking for more than the market is prepared to pay, or the quality of the dwelling is low. My place was in good shape and the rate was competitive.

At the first inspection, a few groups came through and there were two applications. One was a man in his thirties who had been living with his parents. I couldn't judge him for that, but his former employer didn't exactly give a glowing reference. The second application came from a 22-year-old couple. One was the legal guardian of their seventeen-year-old sibling due to their parents being unable to care for them. Their income was low, but they did have money in the bank. I faced an unexpected internal battle over this. Suddenly I had the power to decide who received a roof over their head and who was rejected. It weighed heavily. I wanted to give the 22-year-olds a go – they'd probably done it tough. But on the other hand, they were young, they were caring for a teenager and they had unstable incomes.

The agent suggested I hold out for more applicants, offering a further midweek inspection option to see if we could attract more people. I agreed with that call and declined both applications, wondering if I'd done the right thing. In the meantime my apartment sat empty while I unpacked (yet again), this time in Richmond.

I was simultaneously searching for a housemate and was looking forward to the company, but after so much time on my own I wanted someone independent. I wasn't seeking a new best friend, I mostly just wanted to reduce my cost of living.

In the short term I offered the room to a friend who was about to move to London, which generated a few hundred dollars to cover the gap while I found a permanent housemate. I placed an ad online and the messages dropped into my inbox. The room was tiny – much smaller than mine – so I set the price at $750 per month. Many people told me this seemed too good to be true, and were quick to inspect. The bargain price attracted travellers and people who wanted to save. It was clear that professionals my age preferred to fork out for better properties with larger rooms. In the end, I chose a guy five years younger than me who wasn't looking to spend a fortune on rent. We sat in the living room and bantered easily. He started work early, so there was no danger of morning bathroom battles. I offered him the room shortly after our meeting.

In the first few weeks we sat on the back deck after work, drank cider, and got to know each other. My friends visited, so did his. Weeknights suddenly had life in them and I was so thrilled that I was prepared to overlook the fact that he was a prolific Tinder operator. Look, he had a personal life, which he was entitled to, but we shared a wall, so sometimes I had to endure the intimate details of his escapades. Often I fell asleep with music blaring in my earbuds to drown out the sound of the activities taking place in the next room.

It seemed like a small price to pay for the advantages of having someone to come home to, though. After a particularly bad day, when I was lying on the lounge feeling sorry for myself, he walked into the living room, dragged me off the couch and made me go for a walk with him. Sometimes a quiet Saturday night turned into a spontaneous gathering – his mates rocking up with drinks and quality banter. I had missed this so much.

But I was also a nag. He used my good wine glasses for water and I pulled him up on this the first time, and the twenty or so times after that. 'These are special to me, they're only for wine,' I'd say. I had to remind him to do his share of the cleaning or put the bins out. Then I'd bring up the wine glass issue again.

And yet, for the first time in years, I was ordering UberEats, going out for dinner and buying clothes without angsting about what I was spending. I was in a position to comfortably pay the gap on my mortgage that the tenant's rental payment didn't cover. Using wine glasses for water wasn't such a big deal, really. I needed to chill out.

Handling tenants

As far as being a landlord is concerned, you can find a tenant privately, without using a real estate agent, in which case you arrange for the tenant to pay you directly – usually a month upfront, as well as a bond that should be held by the bond authority in your state.

Generally, the bond would be the equivalent of one month's rent. The alternative is to select a property manager through a local agent. In this case, the agent will manage your listing, hold inspections, verify the tenant's application and manage the lease agreement. Once the tenant has signed the lease, your property manager will arrange the first month's rent and bond. They'll transfer the rent to you, minus their fee. Fees vary, but to give you an idea: my property manager charges about 6.5 per cent of my monthly rental income. But if your property is negatively geared, these fees are tax-deductible. Plus, I see it as a small price to pay to have someone who can quickly manage any issues that arise on my behalf, especially if I'm busy at work or out of town.

Each month, the payment is deposited in your nominated account. I immediately transfer these rental payments to my offset account so it's there for the bank to take my mortgage payment.

Rental defaults

It's a good idea to have some extra money stashed away, in case rent doesn't drop on time. A few times, my mortgage payment has come out of my account before my rent has been paid. Luckily, I had the extra funds – otherwise I would have been overdrawn or defaulted on my mortgage repayment. I've only ever had rent arrive a few days late, but if for some reason rent wasn't paid I'd have to find the cash to cover the mortgage as well as my own rent while the issue was resolved.

If a tenant doesn't pay rent within fourteen days, they are in arrears, which means you or your property manager can issue a notice to vacate. Before this, you may work with the tenant to understand if this is an isolated incident or an ongoing problem. If it's an ongoing problem, you'll likely expect compensation for unpaid rent. The process to address this varies from state to state. In the meantime, you'll probably be looking for a more reliable tenant.

Property damage

A bad tenant can leave you with unexpected costs. That's why land-lord insurance is essential. Depending on your policy, you'll be covered for damage, vandalism, burglary and loss of rent if your tenant does a runner.

Maintenance

If you're asking for a competitive rental-market price, your property should be well maintained. New properties shouldn't have too many unexpected maintenance costs early on, but as your property ages there may be bills you have to budget for. When I bought Mordialloc, it had new carpets and had recently been painted, but before I moved out I installed a new security door and split-system heating and cooling. I re-grouted the tiles in the bathroom. The place is in good shape, but I still keep a bit of money in my back pocket for unexpected maintenance: this can be something as small as a leaking tap.

If you have a property manager, they'll do routine inspections and check for small maintenance issues that might need attention. If your tenant's lease comes to an end and the property needs updating, it can be good to get in and fix things before you list the property again.

Avos of Wisdom

 If you buy an apartment, get involved in the owners corporation. Make sure you know where your money is going and whether it can be better spent.

 A rentvestor is also a landlord – make sure you understand this responsibility and be prepared to cover costs if for any reason your tenant doesn't pay on time.

 Moving from owner-occupier to rentvestor can take time. Be clear on the costs associated with the process before you commit and get a good sense of the amount of rent that will cover the mortgage, as well as the gap you may need to pay. Factor this in when you choose your new rental.

14

The Big Picture

IN A STUDIO HEATED TO thirty-seven degrees, I limped into downward dog, fell out of my tree pose and collapsed into relaxation. After the hot yoga class finished, I bounced out of the studio with enough time to sit and drink coffee at my local cafe before meandering through Richmond's backstreets to my office.

I'd been accustomed to getting up early for years now, but I'd never stopped resenting the hours spent in the car. On morning commutes, I'd often fantasised about spending an hour exercising before arriving at the office. I made a deal with myself: when I moved, I would continue to rise early and take up regular morning yoga.

Now, settled in my new life in Richmond, I committed to a trial. Having survived my introductory session, I went again the next day, and the next. Yoga became an instant addiction, but I was kidding myself if I thought that a daily practice would compensate for the pressure of working two jobs. It actually meant even *less* sleep than I'd been getting before.

For six months I got up at 5.30 am, went to yoga, walked to the office, worked from around 9 am until 6.30 pm, walked home, then chipped away at my *Australian Financial Review* property work while eating dinner on the couch. I'd try to be in bed by 10 pm so I could do it all over again the next day.

In August 2016 I cracked. After writing executive property listings almost every single week for eighteen months – including the weeks I was on Christmas holidays or annual leave – I just couldn't do it anymore, so I quit. I hadn't paid off as much of my credit cards as I would have liked, but I had a few thousand saved for future bills. Now that my rent was more affordable, I should have been able to save, too.

Did I?

Nah. I spent the next twelve months reclaiming my social life. I bought new clothes, and went out for dinner and to parties. I said yes to every invitation.

I had not been kind to myself for a *really* long time. This has a flow-on effect. Mortgage broker Ben Ong says that financial stress puts incredible pressure on relationships, and that moving away from your work and community adds to that strain. 'The suburbs are where relationships go to die sometimes,' he tells me during one of our chats. That's not the case when people are living where they want, or they're close to where they grew up, or work, but in my case, the suburb I'd chosen was where my relationship with myself had gone to die. Even though I'd now moved to where I wanted to live, I'd made lifestyle choices that had prevented me from enjoying my own company, and if I didn't like spending time with myself, how could I expect anyone else to?

In 2017, I did some soul searching and decided to remove everything from my life that wasn't working. I asked my housemate to move out. It'd been fun, but I was done with the late-night lovers, water in wine glasses and having to nag about cleaning. I quit my job, which I'd loved, but I felt I'd achieved everything I could there. I moved on to something that came with a decent pay rise so I could cover the rent on my own. In retrospect, I see this was a mistake. My mantra had become: *more money, more money, more money.* It should have been: *change your lifestyle so you don't need so much money.*

Don't give up everything you value for home ownership

Saving for a home and surviving that first year of ownership is always going to come with challenges and sacrifices, but I now realise that it's important to decide *which* sacrifices to make and how long you'll make them for before you're able to live comfortably again, or do the things you value and that sustain you. My biggest mistake was giving up too many things simultaneously: proximity to my community, time for myself and my friendships. My career aspirations had been more or less forgotten, too.

In hindsight, I could have waited longer to buy or bought a cheaper, regional investment that I didn't have to live in. I should not have given up on my career goals for a mortgage and I encourage you to explore ways to buy without giving up *all* the things you love.

Non-millennials will roll their eyes at this. In 2016, author Simon Sinek was interviewed on the show *Inside Quest*. He was banging on about the way millennials were raised to believe they could have anything they wanted and, as a result, 'You have a generation growing up with lower self-esteem, that doesn't have the coping mechanisms to deal with stress.' Later, he described our need for instant gratification and the fact that we're basically all ruined: 'You'll have an entire population growing up, going through life and never really finding joy. They'll never really find deep fulfilment in work or life,' he claims.

I'm sorry, what?

I don't know about you, but I'm pretty tired of these arbitrary one-size-fits-all proclamations about millions of people who happen to be born during a certain period. Sure, some kids who've been coddled will struggle when their parents aren't there to give them a cash transfer and a cuddle if things don't go their way, but this can be said of any generation, not just millennials. Personally, what I'm seeing is a generation of creative, remarkable people launching innovative businesses – from tech start-ups to cool cafes. They're having a crack. When they fail, they lick their wounds and they get back up again.

Growing up in the digital age, we've realised that there are countless career opportunities and life trajectories. If we've been spoilt with anything, it's choice. That's where the problem lies. When our parents were young, they were doctors, lawyers, hairdressers, teachers, nurses, tradies or accountants. They weren't founding start-ups, working as social media consultants or propping up the gig economy as freelancers.

It's possible to follow your personal, vocational passion and purchase property, too. Take Tammy Butow. Like most kids, she was pretty stoked to get her first computer. But it was more than a device for games and touch-typing; it unleashed a passion for technology. Tammy worked hard after she graduated from Queensland University of Technology with a Bachelor of Computer Science, becoming an engineering manager with the National Australia Bank. Initially she focused on building her career, but then started saving hard a few years in. At twenty-seven, Tammy purchased a three-bedroom home in Victoria's Yarra Valley. It took her two years to save. 'I didn't spend much during that time or go on any holidays. I had to sacrifice fun to be able to buy a home, but I'm really glad I did,' she says.

But Tammy worked simultaneously on her passion to get more young women into science, technology, engineering and maths. Currently, just 12 per cent of engineers are women. Tammy founded Girl Geek Academy with four other Australia-based professionals. 'I wanted to create a company with friends where we could help other women meet like-minded technical women,' she says. The team works with teachers, schools and start-ups to get women into coding, 3D printing, wearable technology and others working the science, technology, engineering and maths – or STEM – fields, areas where women have traditionally been underrepresented. 'I love being able to meet other smart women, have amazing conversations and cheer them on as they do amazing work,' Tammy enthuses. She's now based in the United States, working for big tech businesses while establishing Girl Geek Academy initiatives there. Tammy has held on to her property despite the move, getting professionals to manage it in her absence. To young people who want to follow a passion and buy property too, she says, 'You can do both. You might have to go out less, but it will only be for a few years.'

Contrary to Simon Sinek's generalised views, there are so many millennials embracing this entrepreneurial spirit. They're doing things they love that are aligned with their values. They're happy because they don't hate going to work every day. If they do hate it, they do something about it. We're not slaves to jobs we loathe for the sake of a mortgage. Smart millennials are setting up lifestyles that enable them to get the most out of every day.

Buying if you're self-employed

But if you're going into business on your own, you do face a specific set of hurdles when it comes to home ownership. It can be a struggle to get a home loan when your income is inconsistent, and you don't have regular payslips to show the bank.

If you run your own business and you're keen to buy a home, it's a good idea to develop a savings history well in advance of your loan application. A strong saving track record, along with well-maintained accounting files, will put you in a better position. Your tax returns will have to be up-to-date, as you'll need to supply your ATO notice of assessment, as well as at least one to two years of business activity statements (BAS), which set out your annual income turnover, and helps your potential loan provider get a better sense of your borrowing capacity.

Even with tidy records, your borrowing capacity may be reduced if your income is volatile. To inhibit the potential risk, you may be required to fork out a 20 per cent deposit, or perhaps even more. So be prepared to hear this news.

That's not always the case, though. It largely depends on how much you're earning and what you're claiming at tax time. Mortgage broker Ben Ong points out that many self-employed people have the capacity to reduce their taxable income by claiming a broader range of expenses. And yet, when it comes time to apply for a home loan, the lender makes decisions heavily focused on taxable income. Ben points to the case comparison of two people earning $75,000 per year, one salaried and one self-employed. 'It's likely that the self-employed person has claimed tax deductions – everything from office materials to home electricity or car expenses – reducing their taxable income, which the banks measure servicing by.' Meanwhile, the person on the salary will likely have fewer deductions, which makes their taxable income higher, subsequently improving the strength of their application.

It's also handy to know that most lenders will review *two years* of taxable income and use either the lower of the two or an average of the two upon which to make their evaluation. 'So, where someone makes $50,000 in year one and then $100,000 in year two, lenders will view the income based on $50,000 or $75,000, with only a small minority basing their assessment on the last year,' Ben explains.

It's a good idea to talk to a mortgage broker like Ben about your options before making an application, as there are so many extra variables for small business owners and sole traders to consider. That's not to say it's impossible, or too complicated, you'll just need to be organised and be able to show that you can manage your money effectively. If you're doing a good job administering your own small company, then you've surely got the chops.

*

People come into our lives for all kinds of reasons. Some make no sense, but when Aaron showed up in my orbit the purpose of his presence was obvious immediately. It was time to get jolted out of my zombie-like, budget-obsessed state and cast my imagination back to the career goals I'd nurtured before I filtered all my energies into getting a home. Aaron arrived at the right time.

My phone lit up while I was sitting at my desk one afternoon, trying to decide which item on my to-do list to turn my attention to next – not one task inspired me. 'Write a story using band names for me,' he texted. I figured he prided himself on sending eccentric messages to reinforce his artistic identity. Whatever his motivation, the creative stimulation was something I didn't know I was so desperately missing.

'Can I use individual artists and pronouns?' I replied.

'Nah, bands. Kiss. The Shins.'

I started mentally listing band names that might be shuffled into a paragraph as my phone glowed again. 'I'll accept Prince,' he added.

'The Killers Panic at the Disco. The Police Go West: Chicago. And Hell Followed With A Flock of Seagulls,' I eventually replied, after extensively googling band names that made sense in a sentence. Once I'd hit send, the epiphany pulsed through me. That little exchange had given me a familiar brain buzz. The sensation had guided me professionally in the past, but it had been absent for so long. When it kicked in, I got so focused that a natural disaster could occur around me and I wouldn't have noticed.

I've done the hard yards. Maybe I don't have to go on doing work that doesn't give me this feeling, I thought. The acute awareness would trigger an irreversible desire to blow up the career I'd built since buying my home. The question was: how did I take action?

Should you use equity to pay off debt?

This process began slowly and methodically in February 2018 with an application to refinance my home loan and dip into my equity to wipe out my credit cards in full. I'd been making minimum monthly credit card payments, about $200 each to this point, but consistently remaining around $11,000 in debt because I was mostly only paying the interest on what I owed. It dawned on me that I probably didn't have to do that anymore.

The application to refinance involved filling out a range of forms indicating how much I needed, what my monthly expenses were and how much I was earning. It's much like any other loan application, except in this case I was using the value of my home as security, which is calculated using the same loan-to-value ratio that's used when you're applying to borrow at the outset. When I bought Mordialloc, I had a high loan-to-value ratio of about 90 per cent because I didn't have a 20 per cent deposit and I was using lender's mortgage insurance, so at that point the bank was never going to give me more money to roll my credit card debt into the loan. Now, however, I'd been paying down my mortgage for four years and my property had simultaneously gone up in value, so my loan-to-value ratio was down to about 70 per cent, making my application lower risk.

When you apply to refinance your loan, the bank will arrange for an assessor to review the current value of your property and check your financial situation to ensure you can manage the obligations of the new loan. For example, if you owe $285,000, a $15,000 loan could put your mortgage back up to about $300,000. While that's not ideal, in my case it meant I'd no longer be making hundreds in credit card repayments with extortionate 12 per cent interest rates.

I asked financial adviser Jess Brady if I'd done the right thing. The Sydney-based thirty-year-old started a business called Fox & Hare in 2017 that aims to help young people get their finances in order.

'It works if you get the capital growth, but if there's no capital growth, you've overextended or bought too early,' she says of refinancing. 'You were able to get into the market,' she explains, and agrees that it was the right move for me at that time because the value of the property rose in the years after I purchased, and I saved on rent because I bought sooner. 'The numbers worked in your favour – there are huge advantages, capital growth and tax benefits, because it's an investment.' 'The caveat being,' she cautions, 'understanding how not to use a credit card in the future.'

Ultimately, you want your equity to stay with you, rather than leaning on it to pay off overspending. Jess says there are scenarios to consider: bad debt, like credit cards, and good debt, which might be a mortgage you owe money on – it's good because it's an asset that you hope will grow in value. In refinancing, what I'd done was convert my bad debt into good debt. But the endgame should be *no debt*, so that the asset actually provides income. For me, that means aiming to have my home paid off so that rent becomes money in my pocket rather than something I use to pay down my mortgage.

Jess points out that my plan wasn't foolproof. Had my property's value remained the same or dropped, I potentially wouldn't have been able to use the equity to pay out my credit card debt. I was lucky, and I made some informed bets.

She highlights a client of hers who wasn't so fortunate. He used his credit card to make up his total deposit for an apartment in Zetland, four-kilometres from Sydney's CBD. He had a 5 per cent deposit and used a personal loan and a credit card to cover the rest of the expenses tied to buying. That gives you an idea of how desperate first home buyers in Sydney were to get into the market before it cooled. Jess says he'd been able to access those kinds of funds because he had a good income and no other liabilities. But she points out, 'The bank must not have looked very closely at his spending behaviours as they would have been able to see fairly quickly he was not saving anything on a regular basis.' Escalating house prices and loose lending put this 36-year-old in a seriously tight spot. If your response to this is *WTF, how did he even do that?* You're not alone. Even Jess can't entirely understand how he used credit to cobble a deposit together. 'Surely not a cash advance ...' she muses.

'He came to me with just over $60,000 in credit card and personal loan debt on a high interest rate, as well as his mortgage,' Jess recounts. Since then, she has structured a cashflow plan for him and worked with his bank to restructure some of the debt into his mortgage as a means to reduce the masses of interest. But not all of the debt *could* be moved into his home loan, because the market has cooled and he doesn't have the equity required. So, although he's living in the apartment and paying down the mortgage, 'he is still stuck paying the higher interest amount for the part of the loan the bank wouldn't structure inside his mortgage,' she explains. He spent a year paying the credit card off.

'To me, this highlights behaviour that is highly emotional and not well thought through,' Jess tells me. She concludes that, 'The best time to buy a property is when you can actually afford it. Don't get into the market and hope everything will work itself out later.' Hearing this story makes me realise how fortunate I was to buy a property that achieved enough capital growth for me to roll my debt into my home loan. It was a risk I didn't completely understand at the time.

A few days after I sent my application to refinance, I received an email to say it had been approved. I returned to the bank to sign the paperwork, and not long after that the money was sitting in my offset account. I paid out both credit cards in full. I closed one and reduced the limit on the other to a few thousand, opting to keep it on hand for absolute emergencies. Finally being free of the shackles of credit card debt left me feeling buoyant. I was making enough to live on and even put away some extra cash. My bank manager told me that soon I could be in a position to borrow against Mordialloc to buy a second property. But the compromise would be that I would remain locked in professional golden handcuffs. No, thank you. I'd had enough.

Jess reckons that's the right approach. She sees people seeking to collect properties and she always asks them: 'What are you buying it for? What's your end goal?' More specifically, do you want a home, or do you want a passive income generated by an investment with good yield potential? 'I find people have not spent the time understanding where they want to go,' she advises. And those without a strategy aren't doing themselves any favours. In my case it was wise not to rush into buying something else. At that point, I still had to work out what I really wanted *for my life*.

Jess reminds me that it's possible to put money into things that are aligned with your values. 'Millennials are far greener and more purpose-driven than previous generations. We're seeing that in their investments,' she says. Through 'ethical investment', you can do good and get a return, too. It gave me something to think about: personal values and investment weren't necessarily mutually exclusive.

Finally, I'd given myself permission to relax. Except I wasn't relaxed. I'd forgotten how to. Fight or flight mode had been activated for so long it was now my permanent setting. Back in September 2017, I'd left The Royals for a job that paid more, convincing myself it was time to move on. I'd been there for three and a half years. This was a step up in my career in terms of pay and seniority, but honestly it was mostly about the money. Reflecting on it, I quickly developed that sinking feeling that I'd stuffed up.

The discomfort made way for reflection. I'd taken a job in advertising when I bought my apartment because I needed it, desperately. The moment I made that commitment, every subsequent decision was premised on how much money I could make. I wandered so far off my chosen path, propelling myself forward in the name or mortgage repayments rather than meaningful personal achievements, and I hadn't even noticed. I'd become such a master of faking enthusiasm for tasks that weren't even close to what I'd aspired to do at the beginning of my career, that I had fooled myself. Or was this just the reality of growing up and taking on more adult responsibilities? I had assumed it was.

Yet there was Aaron – bursting at the seams with enthusiasm for his art. Consistently motivating me to find passion in my days. Like a child asking 'but why?' at every conversational turn, he challenged my pragmatism and cynicism relentlessly. It was both impressive and annoying, because I knew he was right to question my attitude. It forced me to ask myself what I was passionate about and why I wasn't doing work aligned with that passion. And to wonder, again, if – and how – I could.

Although juggling the property column for the *AFR* had been a battle, I'd loved writing it and had continued to follow property market news. I'd noticed that all of the real estate websites were posting story after story about millennials being shut out of the market, a topic I understood intimately, so I started tinkering away at a blog with the aim of inspiring people like me to find ways to buy a home. Hours evaporated when I worked on it. Even if I'd already spent a long day at work, writing up the stories of other people who were busting their arses to succeed fuelled my fire.

Choosing a career that's a passion is a luxury, especially for a generation that has to work so hard just to get by. I'd made choices that had helped me to achieve my goal, but I'd given up a lot of who I was to do it.

The awakening that followed occurred slowly. It's pace was not dissimilar to the burnout that was tightening its grip on my insides. Sluggish, but all-pervasive, moving at the pace of a snail, but shuffling forward nonetheless. I'd become a robot: saying the right things at the right times in meetings, insisting on improving processes, highlighting inefficiencies, then going home and sinking a bottle of red to dilute the nervous anxiety pulsing through me, but finding it only enhancing the numbness that sat alongside that unease. How long would it take for me to admit I simply wasn't being true to myself? At this point the main thing keeping me going was fear: of what would come next, of what might go wrong, of not making enough money, of having to sell my apartment if I made the wrong choice. But even the fiercest fear couldn't override my sense that something even bigger was missing. My body knew; my mind just had to catch up.

By July 2018, I was hitting the snooze button until the last possible moment. I could no longer muster the motivation to rise for yoga. When I did eventually emerge from under the sheets, reluctantly, I didn't rush to make up lost time. I wandered in to work when I'd found the energy to put on my professional face. The work wasn't the problem: I was. I had nothing left to give. I was officially burnt out.

A year prior to that, my friends Beau and Kim – the ones I spent weekends with while saving – had moved to Ireland. Kim was from a small town in the Kilkenny County called Graignamanagh, and she wanted their children to experience her home and know their cousins. They'd told me I could come and stay whenever I liked. I had some savings, an impending tax return and zero debt. It was the anniversary of their departure and I realised there was nothing stopping me from joining my dear friends in Ireland.

My brother Joel had offered to move into my Richmond rental for three months and get a mate in to rent the other room while I travelled. With that locked in, I handed in my notice. My plan was to revive my freelance writing practice while travelling. This is not something a financial adviser would ever recommend. But this wasn't a financial decision, it was about living.

It turns out that the best thing about purchasing an investment instead of a home is that it can simply sit there, quietly doing its thing, while you find your groove – or get your groove *back*, or whatever – which is something you definitely might have to do after the efforts involved in personal property acquisition. Jess calls this being 'location independent'. She has a number of clients who've bought investments so they can have a property without giving up their freedom. One client has bought in Sydney while building a career in New York.

Hustling for more than four years to purchase and sustain an investment property had given me room to move again. I packed my belongings, wrapping precious items in newspaper once again, this time moving them into storage. I turfed wheelie bins full of junk I'd accumulated over the years and put a select curation of items in a suitcase. It's amazing how little you need when you're ruthless. As I prepared to board the flight to Dublin, I felt I was making a move that would bring me back to life after years of running on autopilot.

Avos of Wisdom

 Know what your end goal is when you're entering the market. A good financial adviser might be able to help you develop a long-term strategy. Don't be afraid to revisit – and potentially revise – this goal as circumstances and opportunities change.

 If you develop equity in your home over time, you might use it to pay off debt, but this is not something that can be relied on. Check in with yourself regularly.

 We all grow, change and wander on and off the path we want to be on. If the goalposts have moved or you're not being true to yourself, give yourself time to stop and think about how you can recalibrate.

15

Growing Your Portfolio

THE TIME IT TAKES TO get a second investment is determined by two things: how fast you can save more money, and how fast you can build equity in the property you already own. If you're relying on equity through capital growth alone, it's probably going to take longer. If you add value to your home through a renovation, for example, you can quickly boost the worth of your asset. But, even if your equity spikes through a refurb or changing dynamics in your purchase suburb and you think you have the resources to fund a second property, you need to be sure you can service the second loan on top of the one you already have.

Financial adviser Jess Brady says using equity to renovate can make sense, but not always. She highlights one couple who had three investment properties and wanted to spend a total of $100,000 renovating and refurbishing them. When they ran the numbers, they found that while this would increase rental return a bit, it would take eight years of rent to get that money back – 'it didn't make commercial sense.' This is another instance where raw figures might help to counter emotions.

Particularly for the types of investors considering improvements to their property because they care about good maintenance and want their tenants to be happy, it's essential to work out how much these will ultimately increase your rental yield and how long it will take to get a return.

It's different if you're renovating to sell. To first home buyers purchasing a fixer-upper with the aim of making a profit, she says, 'Look at the things that are easily fixable' and avoid properties that are going to cost hundreds of thousands to repair. Ultimately, you want to minimise your risk: if you overspend on a renovation, you're going to reduce the profits you make in a sale.

Turning lemons into lemonade

Emily Lynch and her partner, Jack, don't muck around. After buying a one-bedroom unit in Melbourne's inner suburb of Kensington for $330,000 in 2016, they've already traded up and have taken on a serious home renovation a little further north in Coburg. But the journey has been far from breezy.

In her limited spare time, 27-year-old Emily is studying marketing at RMIT, while working full-time as a senior property stylist. Jack, twenty-eight, is a personal injury lawyer. 'The biggest challenge is not being taken seriously because of our age,' she says. They missed out on a lot of homes before making an offer on the Kensington property prior to auction.

The couple met while studying law and bonded over shared values and aspirations. 'When we started dating, we didn't go out spending $500 a week having fun,' Jack recalls. They come from similarly hardworking families. 'We didn't get everything we wanted as kids,' Jack says and believes that's what sets them apart from other people their age.

To get their first place, they used a 20 per cent deposit they saved together. They borrowed the stamp duty, which meant they paid lender's mortgage insurance. 'We lived there for more than eighteen months, did a minor renovation and styled it for sale last year,' Emily recounts. 'We are very good savers. While we don't necessarily go without, I account for every expense and plan a lot.'

That's an understatement. Emily allocates money to everything from groceries to hair appointments and knows where every cent goes. The pair has a system that allows them to splurge a bit on the weekend, but during the week they live on a 'uni budget'. They worked on paying down their mortgage while living in the apartment, listing it on Airbnb and then either staying with family in country Victoria or renting cheaper rooms on Airbnb when it was booked. 'This enabled us to throw loads of extra money onto our mortgage every month,' she says. They sometimes made enough to cover repayments in a matter of days, by listing the place during the Spring Racing Carnival, for example, or during the Royal Melbourne Show, which is held at the nearby Showgrounds.

'When we sold, we got a great return, surprisingly, as the apartment market can be quite unpredictable and several other places were for sale, or still are, in the same building,' Emily says. She attributes their luck to both their renovation and the home styling which she pulled off through her work. 'I really think it was all the personal touches that made it stand out from the crowd.'

The house they bought next wasn't what they'd planned. Jack's parents had purchased the Coburg property as an investment ten years earlier and were ready to sell. Jack and Emily engaged two valuations and agreed to buy the home for a price that sat in between the values. They forked out a bit more than a million dollars in May 2017, using a 10 per cent deposit from their apartment sale topped up with lender's mortgage insurance so they could keep some reserve renovation funds at the ready. After they paid the $65,000 stamp duty, they were left with about $65,000 for the refurb. 'We also live off one wage mainly to support us and pay our mortgage,' Emily explains. 'The other goes into our renovation fund. So, we see that topped up by around $800 a week.'

Some might perceive this direct market access to a parental asset as an unfair advantage, but Emily says: 'While we did have the opportunity to buy a place without an auction, it certainly wasn't any easier. Having missed out on many auctions before, we stepped our budget up to buy this place.'

We're standing in their renovated kitchen in the Coburg house and it's easy to see why they're so damn proud of their achievements. The white-tiled splashback and perfectly installed cabinetry is superb. Like anything that's hard-won, they appreciate it more because it's been a slog. 'Jack got a bit "demo-happy", knocking out the kitchen pretty early on,' Emily smiles. She identifies living without cooking facilities as easily the biggest challenge. How did they survive? She points to the Thermomix that now has pride of place on their kitchen bench. 'We had it set up in our bedroom on our dressing table,' she says. 'My parents live in Flemington. If we were desperate, we'd go over there and have food that was cooked in an oven.'

Although they've invested heavily, Emily and Jack believe the renovation will put them in front. 'Our last apartment showed us that if you spend the right amount of money on a home, you will get it back,' Emily points out.

But this one has been a bigger undertaking than anticipated. 'We initially thought there wouldn't be too much work. A slap of paint, new kitchen and bathroom and we would be done. However, every job seems to have ten other jobs joined to it,' Emily says. Jack explains that the key to staying sane was completing work in stages. 'We'd do about three months at a time, get over it and want to spend our money on other things for a while.'

Here's what they've tackled: a restumping, replastering, a new kitchen, opening up the living area, new floorboards sourced from

a demolished Californian bungalow (followed by sanding and pol-
ishing said floorboards), painting, and a new bathroom and laundry.
Their first renovation had been a lot simpler, so a lot of this work was
uncharted territory. It was a big learning curve. 'We knew what we
were supposed to do and in what order,' Emily says, but she admits
there was plenty of internet research. 'We have YouTubed how to
silicone and how to patch areas and holes. Tradies share that stuff
online,' she explains, saying there's never been a better time to try
DIY because there are excellent tutorials everywhere. But even the
most gung-ho DIYers know when its time to engage specialists for
serious jobs, like the floor-to-ceiling tiling in their ensuite. It looks
seriously luxurious. There's a double showerhead. Another hot tip
from Emily: they scoured trading websites to find quality fittings at
affordable prices. Emily points to the window above the sink: 'That
was $50 on eBay.'

In 2019, they took the renovation outside, adding a new deck, a
driveway and landscaping the garden. For months, they lived in the
front room of the house and chipped away, with an hour or so of work
each night before bed. 'Crazy, we know. It just allowed us to go out on
Saturday or Sunday arvo rather than work all weekend,' Emily says.
But the worst is over – they're no longer spending weekends covered
in dirt and dust. 'It feels like that light is almost there and we'll move
to doing new things,' Emily says. Now that the house is looking pre-
sentable, people have come to visit and said, 'Oh my god, how did you
do this? I'll never have this.' But it's not something that just happens.
'We bought a really crap apartment and we renovated it. We got it for
a bargain because no one else wanted it. Everyone has to buy something that isn't their dream before they can get to what they really
want,' Emily believes.

If you're working as a couple, play to your strengths. Emily has the
visual nous, so they physically taped out spaces to be sure they were

on the same page before they went knocking walls over. Regardless of how strong your vision is, it's essential to be kind to each other. 'As much as I'd like to say it's not taxing on a relationship, it really is. We are more tired, slightly grumpy from time to time and it always comes out on demolition days,' Emily admits.

Nonetheless, it pays if you're committed to a common goal. 'Be smart, buy the worst unit, low-cost flip and sell it. Repeat until you have a big enough deposit for what you want long term,' she concludes. To people considering doing the same, Emily has some simple advice: 'Focus on the short term. Buying a few lemons and turning them into lemonade is essential to be able to land a dream property. I think as millennials we sometimes focus on the long-term luxurious goal and forget how much we need to do to get there.'

The fine art of flipping

'Flipping' a house – that is, buying a place that needs work, giving it a makeover and putting it back on the market at a higher price than you paid – is one of the fastest ways to make solid cash from property. Tim Gauci, commercial director at Design + Diplomacy in Melbourne makes a living out of it. He and his partner Nicole Langelier have been so successful they now have agents coming directly to them and asking for help prepping properties before they're listed. Tim reckons there are some simple tricks of the trade that can help to maximise the value of a property. If you want to give it a crack, here's what you need to know.

Buy the right place

This may seem obvious, but it's essential to buy in an area where there's growth, and to pick a property in the best street you can possibly afford. When Tim walks through a property to assess the potential there's a number of things he looks for. 'We make sure there's nothing structural or permit-based that needs to be dealt with.' Ultimately, you want to improve what's there rather than having to do too much heavy lifting. That also means looking to avoid the types of problems that might put buyers off, like damp, mould and termites.

Once they're satisfied a place has potential, they put a scope of work together. Tim says the key is not to get too emotional about the work or inject too much of your own taste: 'It's not a forever renovation, it just has to be campaign-ready.'

Prepare for the 'bag drop' moment

A 'bag drop' is when a prospective buyer walks in to inspect and can see nothing that needs to be done. Tim says you need to make it appealing to a broad demographic without overinvesting in a renovation. He works on a lot of Melbourne's inner-city homes in the million-dollar range and advises spending as little as possible to get the biggest impact. 'In Fitzroy and Collingwood, $30,000 will make a ratty terrace ready.'

For a bathroom, make sure the waterproofing is good and replace the shower and vanity. This shouldn't cost much more than $1500 to $2000. A new toilet is only going to set you back $450, too. In the kitchen, ideally you'll only need to replace the cabinet doors and benchtops. 'You can do a good facelift for between $3000 and $4000,' he says. In terms of light fittings, they replace old bulbs with downlights, and if that's not an option, he'll seek out feature pendant lights. 'If we're lucky and the house is on a slab, we'll do polished concrete floors,' Tim says. Failing that they'll strip the floorboards and repolish. Carpet is also an option. For painting interiors, keep it simple. Tim says an antique white is best. For the property's facade, select something that's contemporary and isn't polarising. You might choose a bold front door, but only if you're in a suburb where that's appealing. Finally, 'make sure the garden is tidy.'

Just like that, a $30,000 spend can turn into a $300,000 profit. Among his team's biggest challenges was 147 Easey Street in Collingwood, the scene of two brutal murders in 1977. When they were called in to flip that home, there were still remnants of the crime.

Flip fast

When you're done with the reno, you'll need to style the house, which might mean investing in professional staging. 'We plan the look around what colour paint we use and the carpet colour we're working with,' Tim says.

'Cosmetic renovating of a property you're living in is a nightmare. It can be better to spend three to four weeks living somewhere else and put it straight back on the market,' he advises. Although that depends on where you've bought. 'In Fitzroy, Collingwood and Richmond, it's not ideal. If it was on *Domain*, people will wonder why it's on the market again, so you might be better to wait for a new season and new buyers,' he concludes.

Avos of wisdom

 It can be tempting to buy a real fixer-upper to significantly improve the value of a property, but those places take a lot more work. Make sure you know what your strengths and weaknesses are and be prepared to outsource professional jobs like electrical and plumbing work. It might be more prudent to find something that requires a less extreme makeover but will still yield a worthwhile profit.

 If you're renovating with the aim of selling, work towards broad appeal. Designing with your own specific needs and tastes in mind might reduce your pool of prospective buyers.

 Look for properties that need the type of cosmetic work that won't break the bank, rather than huge jobs that require structural change.

16

Taking Charge of Your Financial Future

IMAGINE SLEEPING IN YOUR CAR because you've left a violent relationship and you've got nowhere else to go. You've got a job and you were renting with your partner, but you couldn't stay there. Private rentals have become incredibly expensive and funding a one-bedroom place on your own is going to be tight, if not impossible. Even if you can afford it, when it comes time to fill out the application form, you don't have a fixed address, so your application is quickly overlooked. This happens. It's happening right now.

More than twenty-two years ago, a small group of women recognised the need to provide vulnerable people with long-term affordable housing solutions. The women formed a company that later became Women's Property Initiatives. In 1996, at a time when other community housing programs relied entirely on government funding, WPI worked with developers and private sector organisations to raise additional capital. By the early 2000s, they'd completed eleven houses in Roxborough Park, 20 kilometres north of Melbourne's CBD.

Jeanette Large joined the team in 2005 as a part-time development manager and climbed the ranks to become CEO. Having worked in homelessness previously, she understood the growing demand for stable housing and the circumstances of those in need of it. Today they have eighty-three houses and another ten in the pipeline. The women who are housed pay 30 per cent of their household income in rent, and never more than 75 per cent of the market rate. They house women from a range of backgrounds, including refugees and their families. Residents range in age from their twenties to their seventies. Jeanette says 'its not enough to meet demand'.

'The over fifty-fives are becoming a much larger cohort than ever before,' she observes. 'Many of those women would never have thought they might become homeless.' But it only takes one unexpected turn: job loss, divorce or a health problem. 'They're suddenly confronted with the fact that they don't have the income that they used to have and surviving in the private rental market is not feasible.' She highlights the fact that the Newstart allowance pays just $279 per week. Alternatively, the aged pension is $415 per week. 'If you're wanting to have a rental property, pay your utility costs, your food … it's shocking,' she says.

To people who aren't sure if they'll ever afford a home, Jeanette insists it's essential to contribute as much as possible to super. Employer superannuation contributions weren't made compulsory until 1992, so many boomers are now retiring with little to no super. Many millennials in full-time salaried roles have at least had the advantage of compulsory employer contributions from the beginning of their careers.

When people have access to long-term affordable housing, they get more than a secure roof over their heads. 'They have improved health outcomes – both mental and physical,' Jeanette says. They are also more likely to be work-ready because they have stability. 'There are improved academic outcomes for children and improved family relationships. Parents start to focus more on the parenting rather than worrying, "Where the hell are we going to live?"'

About a third of Australia's households are comprised of renters and those numbers are on the up. 'Other countries have always had a much higher rental component, but it's not twelve-month leases.' Jeanette believes more must be done to protect tenants' rights. In places where long-term rental agreements are in place, tenants at least feel like they have a permanent home. Continuously moving is not going to be an attractive prospect for millennials, especially as they move into their forties and fifties. Jeanette thinks that without measures in place to protect tenants we'll only see more problems in the future. While property prices plateaued in Sydney and Melbourne in 2018 before rising again by July 2019, they've remained strong in other cities, and persistent population growth will only continue to elevate demand. 'In Victoria we're still growing by 2000 people a week,' she says.

Builder Sally Wills argues that Australians have to make a massive mental shift in order to truly embrace affordable housing. 'Think big, live small' is her motto. Originally from Melbourne, Sally spent about sixteen years working in Western Australia, project managing and designing large home builds. 'People were telling me they wanted to do something sustainable and energy-efficient and yet they were wanting me to design four-bedroom houses with three bathrooms and two living rooms,' she says. While working on these massive homes, she began to consider a market for alternative dwelling types.

Sally started Small Change Design after returning to Melbourne and completing a building design course at Melbourne Polytechnic (formerly NMIT). 'I started getting the idea that small is better than big,' she says, although there was a surprising amount of opposition to this idea from some sectors of the property industry. 'Most builders and architects will say no one wants that; most real estate agents will tell you the same thing,' she says. Yet she reckons that demand for her properties from prospective buyers is significant. It's easy to see why. Her own petite home in the Geelong suburb of Norlane is awesome.

Arriving at the bright orange front door, I'm already envious that I didn't think to do something this clever. Sally's place has polished concrete floors, a light living room, study nook, bathroom and a cheeky loft hidden above the kitchen. It feels massive despite the fact that it's only 57 square metres. This is thanks to Sally's clever use of space and her A-shaped ceiling design, which is much higher than the standard 2.7 or 3 metres. Although banks have traditionally been hesitant to lend on properties that are less than 60 square metres big, she's had no issues. While this problem still may arise for apartment buyers, a small home on its own title is a different story.

After buying her block for $70,000 a few years ago, she brought one of her designs to life and hasn't looked back. The street is gradually morphing into an exhibition of Sally's work – she designed the home across the road and her next-door neighbour's, too. There's only one problem. Demand for her work has been limited by the Victorian government's restrictions on the building of secondary dwellings on existing titles. Regulations can vary from council to council, but generally a small dwelling or granny flat must be removed if its resident dies or moves out. The reason she's been able to build her own small home on a little plot of land is because she bought a subdivided block. In other parts of Australia, the rules for secondary dwellings are more progressive, so Sally tends to work with clients in other states such as Queensland, where there are more opportunities to build sustainable small homes on big blocks.

Sally continues to lobby the Victorian government, arguing that we need to allow density to occur in suburban backyards. 'The big problem is the land. That's the message I've been trying to get to the government. You can come up with all sorts of innovative building products and different ways of doing housing – prefabrication, small homes – but if there's no land, that's the biggest component cost-wise,' she points out.

Her prospective customers are boomers and millennials alike. The boomers want to build a second property in their backyard and rent out their primary home, so they don't have to leave the area they love, while the millennials are trying to find property that's cheap enough to do a new build on. But that's hard. 'I get a lot of calls from young people,' Sally says; 'They say, "I've found a piece of land, I'm about to buy it, but it's $300,000. So, I've only got $100,000 or $50,000 to build".' That's not enough. People need to get hold of parcels worth $150,000 or less, she suggests, because they're going to spend another $150,0000 to $200,000 to put a home on it, even if it's small. Sally's adamant about the power of putting second dwellings on titles as one of the solutions to the housing affordability problem. 'The advantage is they share services and you don't have subdivision costs. That would help a lot of people,' she says. Sally has started a change.org petition to amend current planning laws to allow up to 60-metre-square permanent second dwellings on residential titles. Getting this over the line would finally allow Victorians to catch up with the rest of the nation. Sally reckons it's a no-brainer. To her mind, putting more homes on suburban quarter-acre blocks has many advantages.

For starters, 'It's a way of getting more density in the middle suburbs, where they're still very anti-development.' She points to 'Save our Suburbs' campaigners who push to protect areas from medium- and high-density development in a number of Australian states. Wanting to minimise large apartment complexes is one thing, but Sally says there has to be compromise somewhere, as cities continue to grow. Increasingly, she's taking calls from people in the suburbs with millennial kids who can't afford a home. 'Suddenly the ones that were complaining about development in their area are saying a secondary dwelling would be good.'

To those who still oppose subdivision and secondary dwellings, Sally says, 'Sure, you've got a nice suburb, but you're probably going to have to move over a bit and make some room.' She's adamant that we need more good housing around the $300,000 to $400,000 mark, and that it should be 'good quality, sustainable, in places that people want to live'. 'If you take into consideration the average wage, take what people can afford to borrow, then that's what we need to be building. It's so obvious to me.' Endless urban sprawl isn't the solution. 'People are complaining about commutes and traffic, but if you fix the problem of where you put people, suddenly the traffic issues are reduced.'

Sally believes the developers who do continue working on new estates in outer locations need to review the way they design if they want to attract younger residents. 'There's a lot of young people that wouldn't be caught dead in those houses,' she says. 'The builders and developers are so locked into the way they've always done it,' she notes, suggesting they take more cues from inner-city design trends. 'People are saying we will go quite small if we can have something that's nice. We don't mind small if we have a nice kitchen.'

In Sally's experience, design, affordability and lifestyle are the main reasons why young people seeking small, affordable homes are choosing regional locations instead of newly created fringe suburbs. It's no surprise to me to hear that people like me would prefer to live further out, in established towns with character, country pubs, wineries and express train services to the city. That's why they're contacting her in big numbers.

Improving your superannuation and savings

If you still feel like home ownership is well out of reach at this stage in your life, there are many things you can do to improve your financial position over time. For starters, opening a high-interest bank account and putting small amounts in it regularly can help you start to build savings. If you put away even just $20 per week every week, that's more than $1000 per year and more than $10,000 in a decade, plus interest. With those funds, you could invest in shares, or continue building towards a deposit.

If your employer is doing the right thing, you should have the advantage of compulsory saving through regular superannuation contributions – it's 9.5 per cent of your income and it's invested on your behalf, so the figure grows over time. When you start a job, it can be tempting to let your employer elect their chosen super fund, which means you might end up having money stashed in multiple places. Spend a few minutes making sure it's all consolidated into one account. To do this, you'll need a myGov account. Log in and scroll to the ATO section to see all of your super accounts. From there, it's easy to roll your super into a single preferred account. You might also consider making additional voluntary superannuation contributions through your employer. This is known as salary sacrificing. It can improve your position because it means you pay less tax while improving your retirement prospects.

Building financial independence as a team

As a child, Lyndall Murray and her sisters had no idea her parents were doing it tough. 'We had new shoes and uniforms like the other kids,' she recalls. But after their mum passed away when Lyndall was a teenager, she was soon exposed to the reality of her family's situation. 'My parents sacrificed their financial future for us to get the best start in life,' she says. This realisation would become the foundation for her unwavering commitment to financial independence.

After completing an economics and marketing degree at Southern Cross University, Lyndall, who's now thirty-four, moved to Sydney, where she worked for organisations such as the NRL, the AFL and Village Roadshow. But the big city wasn't a place where she could settle. 'Deep in my heart the northern rivers felt like home, so I knew I wanted to return and buy a house in the region.'

While she was adamant she must build her own nest egg, and not rely on the support of a partner, Lyndall wasn't closed to the possibility of love. 'I believe my mum is my guiding light and she sends subtle signs when I need them,' she says. When Lyndall took a seat next to thirty-four-year-old Jono Waghorn on a flight from Exmouth to Perth, the fact that it was her mum's birthday was a subtle nudge in the right direction. The fateful seat allocation would lead to a romance and eventually an unconventional property partnership.

Well before they met Lyndall had been working hard to achieve her financial goals. In 2014, she moved out of a home she had purchased with her ex-boyfriend and recovered slightly less than the $30,000 she'd invested. To save for her own property, she moved to a Byron Bay sharehouse and spent $180 per week on rent. 'I hadn't lived in a sharehouse since my early twenties so it was a transition that felt regressive, but I had a goal to buy my own property and this was part of the sacrifice,' she reflects.

Later, she moved to a $360 per week studio and continued to save as much she could. Jono, who's from Victoria, would come and visit. He was already in the property game, renovating a home on the Mornington Peninsula. 'At the time I was considering buying a townhouse just north or south of Byron within a 45-minute drive, but after striking a deal with Jono that would see him renovate the property I eventually bought in exchange for rent-free living, this shifted the type of property I was looking for,' Lyndall says.

'From January 2017 to July 2017 I knuckled down, saving every penny I possibly could.' But, she adds, 'I managed to balance this with picnics on the beach with mates instead of nights out on the town.' At that time she was looking at townhouses in Lennox Head and Byron Bay that wouldn't require renovation. But the urge to work on a project together grew with her relationship. 'Jono had just finished his own stunning renovation on a property in Rye on the Mornington Peninsula, so I knew he had a talent for transformative renovations,' she says.

Lyndall, a former customer experience director at a tech start-up now runs her own consultancy connecting purpose-driven brands with influencers, and Jono, who's an electrician, are refurbishing a beach shack on the New South Wales coast. But unlike many couples, Lyndall bought the property independently, with her own $100,000 deposit, while Jono works full-time renovating it between construction contracts.

After missing out on a property in Clunes, just inland from Byron Bay, the pair returned their focus to coastal areas and found Evans Head, a 50-minute commute from Byron. Lyndall is certain a highway build currently in progress will reduce the commute to 35 minutes and hopefully add value to the area, too.

Their first estimate was that the property was worth about $470,000. But asbestos removal would be pricey – $18,000 – so they used that as a bargaining tool, eventually settling on a sale price of $457,000. They used Lyndall's $100,000 deposit to secure it in July 2017.

'We spent the first nine months pulling down walls to create open spaces, removing the asbestos and replacing the roof. If I ran out of money, we defaulted to doing the jobs that didn't require a lot of cash,' Lyndall explains. When funds were low, Jono converted the old garage into a self-contained studio so they could stop renting. They moved in there in March 2018, and planned to put the space on Airbnb once the renovation is complete. This is Lyndall's 'first renovating rodeo', but after transforming a dilapidated, beehive-infested 1970s beach house in Rye, Jono is suitably qualified. They engaged asbestos professionals to remove the toxic waste ($18,000) and a roofing specialist for the roof reconstruction ($9000), but Jono otherwise did everything himself. It also helps that 'Gumtree is Jono's best friend', according to Lyndall. He's sourced free materials, including mature golden palm trees – even their new puppy Chilli is a Gumtree find. 'I probably underestimated how hard working full-time on a start-up tech business and renovating a property is,' Lyndall says, 'but Jono has always had my back and supported me and the project when stress levels were very high. I'm very grateful for his calm and logical support.'

'We've turned an old washing machine drum into a makeshift fire pit. On Fridays we burn a fire, have a beer and reflect on the week. In the future when I'm cooking in the completed kitchen and enjoying the adjoining deck, I think I'll look back on these days as making the experience,' Lyndall says. They have an excellent relationship. 'Jono fully supports my goal of financial independence,' Lyndall says.

What if they had to sell, though? 'There was never any discussion about how we would split profits. He would say the house profits are mine,' Lyndall says. Technically Jono could have a defacto claim on the property, but Lyndall says, 'He genuinely wanted to help me secure my financial future, whether we're together in the future or not.'

Although they've so far accumulated assets independently, the have set up a joint bank account for food, date nights and general expenses. Moving forward, they will look at investments that achieve the best outcome for both of them. 'If I was to sell the property, we would make future financial decisions based on this framework,' she adds.

The long-term plan is to stay in the home. They upgraded from the converted studio to the house later in 2018. 'Jono didn't get to live in his Rye house after transforming it. He moved to Byron to start a life with me. Lyndall predicts 'enjoying the fruits of his labour for a few years', though they've also talked about eventually 'getting rid of the bank', selling both properties and taking on a new project. Currently, Jono is living expense-free, but they'll review the scenario when it comes time to pool resources. Renovations are yet to be completed, but even with about $20,000 worth of work still to be done, a recent appraisal valued their place at $600,000. 'I actually collapsed in the hallway when I read the email,' Lyndall says.

If the couple's story has you scrolling coastal listings right now, Lyndall is encouraging but practical: 'Do it, but within your means.' She believes too many millennials get caught up in city home ownership and overstretch themselves to get into the market. 'My advice is to look for a career pivot that might allow you to work remotely. Reduce your mortgage overhead, it'll help bring balance to your life. And don't be afraid of the commute – podcasts are your friend. The time in the car can be used to expand your mind.'

Lyndall is a massive advocate for women securing their own financial freedom but points out that that doesn't mean you have to go it alone forever. She does believe that it's essential to go into relationships with eyes wide open and choose a partner who's capable of frank conversations about money and who supports your personal goals. 'Make sure you have a deep sense of self and that your partner amplifies your love for life,' she concludes.

Avos of wisdom

 Take a leaf out of Sally's book and consider how much space you really need – a small home can be a great home.

 Like Lyndall, you can save on your own and build wealth as a team later. Regardless of your relationship status, it's important to take responsibility for your own finances.

 Even if you're not buying property in the near future, ensuring your super is sorted and understanding where your money goes is a good start.

17

What's Ahead?

AUSTRALIA'S PROPERTY PRICES CLIMBED SO high in recent years that governments had to intervene. Between foreign investment and boomers leveraging their homes to buy additional properties, growth appeared unstoppable. Although we're still dealing with the ramifications of that now – and will be for some time – our strong housing market has also insulated us economically when other countries weren't so lucky.

Leonard Teplin, a development company director, says that during the global financial crisis Australia was protected by foreign capital. 'While everybody around the world was struggling to have money in the system, we had investors migrate to Australia,' he explains. Since then, state and federal governments have made it tougher, taxing foreign investors at increasing rates. In 2017, NSW foreign investment tax rose from 4 per cent to 8 per cent, while in Victoria it's 7 per cent. But that didn't curb demand. According to Leonard, these increases have had little impact. 'The extremely wealthy see it as the cost of doing business,' he says. To further tighten spending, the government reduced the banks' capacity to lend to residents, too, resulting in the period of flatness we experienced.

There's a big difference between a market flattening and crashing, though. 'There are too many industries that rely on property,' Leonard says, explaining that that's the reason property will continue to be a reliable long-term investment in this country. Even if you haven't bought property, chances are your superannuation provider has invested in it on your behalf. Our nation's ongoing prosperity relies on a strong property market. It's what our economy is built on and it's what your retirement nest egg depends on.

All of that may be true, but it doesn't change the fact that, as Leonard also points out, 'entry into the market keeps getting higher'. Regardless of future lending reforms or economic shifts, construction isn't going to get any cheaper and wages for construction workers won't go down. As long as those costs remain high, so do prices. Property may remain a solid investment, but cracking that market seems set to remain tough. With that in mind, he says millennials should 'find the cheapest property they can afford'. Although, he cautions, that doesn't mean buying a $100,000 shack in a state they're not familiar with just because their budget allows it. 'People need to invest in areas that they know.'

If you're investing, a reliable rental return is key, as we've seen. Leonard predicts that's unlikely to be an issue in most cities. With fewer and fewer people capable of making a purchase, the need for rentals will remain strong. He adds that first-homeowner grants tend only to fuel demand and don't actually bring the cost of housing down; these benefits are always evolving and they're not something you should rely on. The important thing, he argues, is to save your heart out. 'What are you prepared to sacrifice to get ahead?'

Nerida Conisbee, realestate.com's chief economist, is definitely seeing that sacrifice taking place. 'There's been a big shift from thirty to forty years ago,' she says. Boomers typically bought in the suburb they grew up in or one suburb out if they couldn't afford to buy where their family lived. It was extremely rare for someone who'd grown up in an eastern suburb to buy a property in the west, for example. 'Now there's a lot of movement,' she says. In larger, more expensive cities, there are three distinct types of first home buyers, she observes: new house and land buyers, people moving to regional areas, and apartment buyers.

The first of these, new house and land buyers, are largely first-generation Australians – those with parents who were born overseas. First-homebuyer concessions for new builds can make this kind of buying attractive, but it's essential for people considering house-and-land packages to ensure the area they're helping to pioneer will be supported by good infrastructure and amenities, including transport and schools.

The second batch of first home buyers are the millennials seeking 'land and a great lifestyle' by making the move away from the city. Nerida highlights the Central Coast and Wollongong as hotspots just out of Sydney for people seeking good homes that don't break the bank. 'They're prepared to do the long commute.' Realestate.com.au data shows more activity in places such as Orange, New South Wales. While it's too far for residents to commute to Sydney, the construction, healthcare and retail industries in Orange are attracting new residents. Here, people can get three- to four-bedroom homes for between $400,000 and $500,000. It's places like this that will continue to draw young millennial families.

As for the apartment trend, this has been unfolding in Sydney for some time because of the extremely high house prices, but it's now on the rise in other capital cities too. 'A decade ago it was unusual for a first home buyer in Melbourne to buy an apartment,' Nerida says, but it's increasingly become the go-to. She says developers are aware of this trend and are trying to make their properties attractive to people who want to make these dwellings their long-term homes, rather than just appealing to investors.

Inevitably, millennials are propping up the rental market. 'Ten years ago a quarter of Australians rented, now it's a third,' Nerida says. Not just because they can't afford to buy, but because if you're not rentvesting, a mortgage does tie you down. Some millennials are choosing to put their money into their own businesses instead of being 'saddled with an $800,000 mortgage'. This generation will rent longer before buying, but that's not to say millennials won't ever enter the market. Nerida suggests increasing flexibility in the way we work will continue to affect where and when we buy. 'People can work in different locations without it having a massive impact on their careers,' she says. She often talks to journalists who are freelancing from Hobart, writing for publications all over the country, but drawn to the affordable living and housing in the island state. In the future, Nerida predicts, 'We'll see people renting for longer, so they can do other things. We'll also see people moving to areas that have a lower cost of living, so they can do more interesting things with the money they've freed up.'

Nerida believes a rise in interest rates is on the horizon to compensate for years of historically low figures. New restrictions to finance will also potentially reduce investor activity. In addition, having won the 2019 federal election, the Coalition government will keep negative gearing tax benefits and will offer new incentives for first home buyers, such as the proposed First Home Loan Deposit Scheme. The scheme, in which buyers could purchase a home with a deposit as small as 5 per cent, will be available for up to 10,000 applicants earning up to $125,000 as a single or $200,000 as a couple. Effectively, the government would act like a guarantor, meaning buyers with less than 20 per cent would avoid LMI. It's an acknowledgement of the problem, but with 110,000 people purchasing their first home in 2018 and similar demand in 2019, it won't help everyone.

Plus, there are concerns about offering loans to people with small deposits when we're seeing market stalls and falls – there is the potential for owners buying with a 5 per cent deposit to end up with negative equity, where they might owe more than their home is worth. The counterargument is that if it is a long-term investment and it gets people into the market, they'll hopefully be right in the long run. Either way, it's not a foolproof solution.

While prices aren't predicted to plummet, and have recently started to recover, reduced competition from investors will hopefully level the playing field and give first home buyers a better chance to get something of their own. And while controversial negative gearing will live on for the foreseeable future, those considering rentvesting will at least get the same tax breaks as the boomers who've enjoyed this advantage.

The upside of the housing affordability crisis

Of these three main trends among first home buyers, I suspect regional investment will be the one millennials will be praised for down the track. While on the one hand it might seem wildly unfair that we're being pushed out of the cities we grew up in, on the other it's easy to see why regional housing is among the most desirable of alternatives, particularly as we get older and some of us seek space and safe environments for our kids to run around. The consistent theme among virtually all my interviewees – cracking the property market in different ways – was a desire to maintain a lifestyle that reflected particular values. We aren't a generation that'll put up with jobs we hate until we retire. We'll be – or, at least, I hope we can be – the 'why don't we have both?' generation: building wealth and careers we're proud of without killing ourselves for it. In turn, we'll spend slower, more fulfilling days with the people we love.

Plus, in making the big move out of cities, millennials are helping to reinvigorate tired towns.

At first I thought Rachel Russo was judging me the day I walked into her produce store Udder & Hoe. I'd just come from spending time with Lucy and Nathan, at their transported home in Loch. All I wanted was a soy latte in a takeaway cup to drink on the way home, but Rachel told me her customers drink their coffee in the store or take a ceramic cup with them and return it later. I explained that I was in the area on a day trip and wouldn't be returning anytime soon. Instead of holding my coffee hostage, she handed me the ceramic cup and told me to keep it. What a legend.

Rachel, thirty-three, embodies what she preaches: good health and slow living. After working as a flight attendant in her twenties and consuming city supermarket carrots that 'tasted like water', she and her husband Karl, also thirty-three, wondered what it might be like to get out of town and live regionally. Rachel has a gentle nature and radiant skin. Just looking at her made me crave a green juice. I've since wondered why I was so hell-bent on getting a takeaway coffee. I wasn't in such a hurry. Why didn't I just stop and drink my coffee, enjoy it and savour the moment?

Rachel and Karl were wise in their twenties, together saving a $40,000 deposit and buying their first one-bedroom apartment for $250,000 in Melbourne's beachside suburb of St Kilda in 2008, which they later renovated. In 2011, they sold it for $375,000 and were in a position to upgrade to a $575,000 two-bedroom Art Deco apartment, just one street over from their original place. As a landscape architect, Karl has both design experience and access to a workshop, so they tackled a renovation on that place, too.

During her time as a flight attendant, Rachel was struck by the poor food quality on planes and amount of waste involved in travel. She longed for a career that was more aligned with her interests in sustainability and community. For a complete change of pace, she spent some time working for Tamsin Carvan, founder of Tamsin's Table, a purveyor of long lunches for guests at her home in South Gippsland's Poowong East, using locally grown produce. Driving from Melbourne to help with the sittings each weekend was 'the perfect way to transition', Rachel says. She'd assist where she could in Tamsin's kitchen and help with hosting. On one occasion she worked in the garden and on another she plucked turkeys. Every event was different.

Originally from the country, Rachel found the pull to this environment, its energy and pace, growing stronger. After the birth of their first child, Wilma, in March 2015, Rachel and Karl began to seriously consider life on their own land. Karl was happy with a regional move: he often surfed in Kilcunda on weekends, and though his landscape design work takes him all over the place it could essentially be based anywhere. They listed their St Kilda home, sold it for a tidy $841,000 in 2015, then lived with Karl's parents for a stint before finding their Gippsland rental.

Shopping for land took time, but they had $380,000 to put towards a block. Along the way they found a site for Rachel's dream produce store and renovated that before opening it in 2016. It took until 2017 for them to secure their 100 acres in Woolamai, on the south-eastern tip of Phillip Island, which they nabbed for $500,000. Why such a massive amount of land? Rachel says there's actually not a huge price difference between 10 acres and 100 acres in this part of the world. More space allowed them the potential to evolve.

'We said we'd find the land and make the house work,' she remembers. Said house became a priority after their second daughter, Florence, was born in September 2017. Initially, they had produced their own home design, but after they'd arranged permits for the new build, they heard about a home, originally built in the 1890s, that had been moved from Toorak to Baxter, which is on the way to the

Mornington Peninsula. 'Although it had been sitting there for five years and had birds living in it, it had good bones,' Rachel says. Plus, the owner was flogging it for a mere $30,000.

Like Lucy and Nathan, Rachel and Karl put the house on a truck and moved it to their site, paying $40,000 for transportation. Although it was cheap, this wasn't the quick and easy route: moving a house meant resubmitting revised planning permits, restumping and more. But doing this reflected their philosophy. Rachel teases this idea out: 'We liked the idea of giving something a new life – the recycled aspect of it, which fits into everything else our life is.'

Years prior to their acquisition of the property, the site had been stripped bare. Since taking possession of the land, they've planted 55,000 native trees. 'It took them ten years to clear it and then ten years to burn it all,' Rachel says, relaying the property's story as its been told to her. 'Our land was once home to cool, temperate rainforest and would have been a spectacular sight with tree ferns and lyrebirds,' she laments. Now, they're on a mission to restore the neglected turf to its former glory. The property's steep, undulating hills are exposed to the elements, so it's not ideal farming land. 'We thought the best way to maintain it, stop erosion and protect the native wildlife was to plant it out with natives,' she says, and they've received support from Landcare Australia, Melbourne Water and local nurseries to make it happen.

The home arrived on their land in 2018 and they spent time knocking it into a liveable state, replacing windows and damaged weatherboards. Then they made interior improvements including plastering, painting and tiling. Rachel, Karl and the kids finally settled in 2019. Despite the fact that it had taken four years from selling St Kilda to moving into Woolamai, they quickly well and truly established the lifestyle they were seeking. The Kilcunda store is such a massive success they opened a second one in Loch, the spot where I first met Rachel.

But professional achievement is more than a healthy profit-and-loss statement. For Rachel, much fulfilment comes simply from meeting people, finding out where they're from and sharing her love of fresh produce with them. Rachel says that she got heaps out of life in the city, as did Karl, but missing from it was the 'connection with people, seasons and food'. She knows not everyone's work enables a regional move, but encourages people who want their own home and land to consider it. Not only is it good for 'giving kids space', which is what her own children love, but people can 'get a bit lost' in city life. For Rachel, the move has completely opened her mind. While their property won't be a farm, they'll be able to grow their own food, make a home for animals and potentially generate some income down the track. 'The possibilities are endless,' she says.

In the few years they've lived in Kilcunda and Woolamai, she says things have already changed and new residents are having a positive impact. 'A lot of people are searching for that connection with a slower life after a stint in Melbourne,' she says. She predicts more young people will follow in their footsteps, bringing dynamic and positive transformation to regional towns and villages. 'Untouched areas are going to be hit with entrepreneurial and passionate people who have the vision.'

Making friends with the future

You can't control the future, no matter how financially literate or good with spreadsheets you think you are. I could worry perpetually about property prices, my next tenant, my next mortgage repayment and whether I'll ever be able to afford a home where I want to live, or I can go with the flow.

During my first days in Ireland, I felt myself breathing easy for the first time in years. Beau and Kim lived about an hour and a half from Dublin. The tiny village of Graignamanagh, in County Kilkenny, has a population of about 2000. There's one historic main street with a couple of cafes, a supermarket and a disproportionate amount of pubs, almost always heaving with merry Irish folk sinking Guinness and singing until late. Even the hardware store transformed into a watering hole after dark.

My friends had been able to buy a two-storey, three-bedroom townhouse that cost about $165,000 Aussie dollars, including a renovation. Beau worked as a freelance journalist. They managed a couple of Airbnb properties, one of which was a houseboat that we'd kick back on between bookings. Beau and I spent afternoons working on freelance stories at the local pub, or from their kitchen table while the kids played in the backyard. Later I'd amble through the old streets and over the historic bridge to the local butcher to grab meat for dinner. If a babysitter was available in the evening, we'd walk up to the local pub and listen to live music.

On one of my first outings, Kim advised me not to ask people what they did for a living. No one there cared for discussing employment. Instead, they'd ask, 'What's the craic?' Translated, this is a request to be entertained with an amusing story. As someone who's never struggled to hold a conversation, I found this surprisingly difficult. My go-to opener has always been, 'So, what do you do with yourself?' As if knowing someone's occupation would give me some deep insight into who they were. In this new scenario, my social worth was only as strong as my ability to draw out an anecdote or tell one that had the crowd enthralled. It was liberating to inhabit a space where people's identities weren't shackled to their work.

People danced under the fairy lights in the warm August air. It occurred to me that the carefree Australian 'she'll be right' attitude has been diluted in recent decades, for various reasons, but no doubt in part because housing has become so precarious and difficult to secure.

In Graignamanagh, no one talked about house prices or mortgages or stifling rents, or appeared to be relentlessly anxious about securing a stable roof over their head.

I didn't know what my future would hold when I returned home, but I decided to try to stop fretting about the things that were out of my control. There would always be something to concern me if I allowed it. An unstable freelance career would require a constant tango with change and there would always be financial hurdles of some kind to overcome. But I had put security in place. The point of buying an investment property was to eventually give myself freedom again, and I'd done that. Now I had to be sure my investment, and any fears I had surrounding it, didn't determine my future.

No less than forty-eight hours after I'd returned home, my old boss Dave posted a callout on Facebook for a short-term content writer. A week later I was back at The Royals, making a coffee in the all-too-familiar kitchen, queuing up tunes and bantering with colleagues about the impending footy finals. That role wrapped up, and I continued to work full-time as a freelance writer. Being true to myself seemed to have an almost magical way of opening new doors. Some days, I work until 9 pm, so I'll treat myself to a mid-morning yoga class the following day. I am working on my own terms, doing tasks that are fulfilling, and I'm happy.

My brother Joel is still in Richmond with me and we're living in surprising harmony with our adopted cat, Peach. A couple of decades of practice have really played to our advantage. I'm continuing to work with my fellow apartment owners to further improve the Mordialloc block. Since I bought, old uninterested investors have sold and young people like me have moved in. Keeping our quarterly levies up has built enough savings to do major work. We've updated the external staircase to make it look more modern and we're re-landscaping the garden. Eventually we'll render the building and give the window frames a fresh coat of paint. I really couldn't be prouder of what we've managed to pull off together.

In hindsight, I could have waited longer to buy, but at that time prices were rising fast, with no end in sight. I would have liked to buy a freestanding home, but with my budget I would've needed to go to the city fringe. I'm glad I didn't go any further than I did, and by all accounts I got a good price. I got into the market with the best place I could afford at the time. I hope it helps me take my next step eventually.

My long-term aspiration is to purchase a second property. The young tree-changers I interviewed have been inspiring, and a regional block with a small home on it is tantalising. But this time, whatever I do, I'd like that purchase to *enhance* my lifestyle, not diminish it. I won't do it until I truly feel financially ready to take that leap. And if I have to keep renting where I want to live, so be it. These days my mind is the place I'm focused on furnishing: with good memories and a positive outlook. I've been able to do this while writing this book, meeting remarkable, driven, optimistic millennials, who've hustled hard.

Buying a property isn't easy. It's not meant to be. It's one of the biggest financial decisions you'll make in your life. But I can say it is worth it, not only for the future security it can provide, but also for the personal growth that accompanies it. Most importantly – hopefully, eventually – it's a place you can call your home. It's yours to paint 'millennial pink', if that's your thing. It's hard, there will be shit bits, but it's not impossible. After the sacrifice comes satisfaction. It's been six years since I wept at my thirtieth birthday dinner. Now, instead of faking my way through adulthood with a champagne flute in hand, I can raise a glass and honestly say, 'Cheers, here's to adulting.'

Acknowledgements

A TOTAL STRANGER, Myke Bartlett, kicked off this amazing ride when he read a blog post my mate Stephen had shared. Myke, for putting me in touch with my wonderful agent Alex Adsett, I'm so grateful.

Alex, your infectious enthusiasm has propelled me forward. Thank you for your commitment to this project and for the incredible work you put in to it, which ultimately led me to the team at Black Inc.

And what a team that is: Sophy Williams, Kirstie Innes-Will and Dion Kagan, it's been a thrill to work with all of you. Thank you for your wisdom, sharp eyes and efforts through this process – you've made this book better than I could have imagined. Kate Nash and the publicity team, you've been passionate about this from the start and I'm so appreciative.

Smashed Avocado wouldn't be what it is without the many people who've shared their journeys to property ownership, some inviting me into their homes and tolerating my questions when they'd rather have been painting walls or cooking dinner. I hope readers are inspired by your stories. I know I am.

So many property and finance experts provided time and shared important information for aspiring homebuyers. Thank you to all of you; but, importantly, thank you Ben Ong – the countless coffees, conversations and emails were always met with patience and positivity. I really can't thank you enough.

My early readers and supporters – Rebecca Thistleton, Sally Wright, Stephen A Russell, Beau Donelly, Kim Fenlon, Mary-Jane Daffy and Margot Bourchier – thank you for workshopping early chapters with me. Your faith and your friendship means the world.

Mum and Dad, you've always encouraged me to do the impossible. I wouldn't be writing these words if you hadn't helped me kickstart my proper adult life. Dad, you've spent so many hours helping me make my goals a reality. I am deeply indebted.

Paul and Joel, thanks for living with me for most of our lives and putting up with me as this story played out. Joel, I'm glad you stopped by for a few weeks and stayed for a year – we're better for it.

Finally, Aaron Tyler, you were there when this little idea was just forming and have challenged me creatively from beginning to end. It wouldn't be *Smashed Avocado* without you. Thank you so much.

Index

Index

NICOLE HADDOW is a Melbourne-based journalist. She was the executive property writer for the *Australian Financial Review*. Buying her first home led Nicole to become passionate about helping people enter the property market. She documents alternative methods of purchasing your first home at smashedavocado.net.